Introduction to Machine Learning with R

with R

Rigorous Mathematical Analysis

Scott V. Burger

Beijing · Boston · Farnham · Sebastopol · Tokyo

Introduction to Machine Learning with R

by Scott V. Burger

Copyright © 2018 Scott Burger. All rights reserved.

Published by O'Reilly Media, Inc., 1005 Gravenstein Highway North, Sebastopol, CA 95472.

O'Reilly books may be purchased for educational, business, or sales promotional use. Online editions are also available for most titles (*http://oreilly.com/safari*). For more information, contact our corporate/institutional sales department: 800-998-9938 or *corporate@oreilly.com*.

Editors: Rachel Roumeliotis and Heather Scherer
Production Editor: Kristen Brown
Copyeditor: Bob Russell, Octal Publishing, Inc.
Proofreader: Jasmine Kwityn

Indexer: WordCo Indexing Services, Inc.
Interior Designer: David Futato
Cover Designer: Karen Montgomery
Illustrator: Rebecca Demarest

March 2018:   First Edition

Revision History for the First Edition
2018-03-08:   First Release

See *http://oreilly.com/catalog/errata.csp?isbn=9781491976449* for release details.

978-1-491-97644-9

[LSI]

Table of Contents

Preface

In this short introduction, I tackle a few key points.

Who Should Read This Book?

This book is ideally suited for people who have some working knowledge of the R programming language. If you don't have any knowledge of R, it's an easy enough language to pick up, and the code is readable enough that you can pretty much get the gist of the code examples herein.

Scope of the Book

This book is an introductory text, so we don't dive deeply into the mathematical underpinnings of every algorithm covered. Presented here are enough of the details for you to discern the difference between a neural network and, say, a random forest at a high level.

Conventions Used in This Book

The following typographical conventions are used in this book:

Italic
:   Indicates new terms, URLs, email addresses, filenames, and file extensions.

`Constant width`
:   Used for program listings, as well as within paragraphs to refer to program elements such as variable or function names, databases, data types, environment variables, statements, and keywords.

`Constant width bold`
:   Shows commands or other text that should be typed literally by the user.

Constant width italic

Shows text that should be replaced with user-supplied values or by values determined by context.

This element signifies a tip or suggestion.

This element signifies a general note.

This element indicates a warning or caution.

O'Reilly Safari

Safari (formerly Safari Books Online) is a membership-based training and reference platform for enterprise, government, educators, and individuals.

Members have access to thousands of books, training videos, Learning Paths, interactive tutorials, and curated playlists from over 250 publishers, including O'Reilly Media, Harvard Business Review, Prentice Hall Professional, Addison-Wesley Professional, Microsoft Press, Sams, Que, Peachpit Press, Adobe, Focal Press, Cisco Press, John Wiley & Sons, Syngress, Morgan Kaufmann, IBM Redbooks, Packt, Adobe Press, FT Press, Apress, Manning, New Riders, McGraw-Hill, Jones & Bartlett, and Course Technology, among others.

For more information, please visit *http://oreilly.com/safari*.

How to Contact Us

Please address comments and questions concerning this book to the publisher:

O'Reilly Media, Inc.
1005 Gravenstein Highway North
Sebastopol, CA 95472
800-998-9938 (in the United States or Canada)
707-829-0515 (international or local)
707-829-0104 (fax)

We have a web page for this book, where we list errata, examples, and any additional information. You can access this page at *http://bit.ly/intro_ML_withR*.

To comment or ask technical questions about this book, send email to *bookquestions@oreilly.com*.

For more information about our books, courses, conferences, and news, see our website at *http://www.oreilly.com*.

Find us on Facebook: *http://facebook.com/oreilly*

Follow us on Twitter: *http://twitter.com/oreillymedia*

Watch us on YouTube: *http://www.youtube.com/oreillymedia*

Acknowledgments

It's always been a dream of mine to write a book. When I was in third or fourth grade, my ideal book to write would have been a talk show hosted by my stuffed-animal collection. I never thought at the time that I would develop the skills to one day be shedding light on the complex world of machine learning. Between then and now, so many things have happened that I need to take a moment to thank some people who have made this book possible in more ways than one: Allison Randal, Amanda Harris, Cristiano Sabiu, Dorothy Duffy, Elayne Britain, Filipe Abdalla, Heather Scherer, Ian Furniss, Kristen Brown, Kristen Larson, Marie Beaugureau, Max Winderbaum, Myrna Fant, Richard Fant, Robert Lippens, Will Wright, and Woody Ciskowski.

```
head(mtcars)
```

```
##                    mpg cyl disp  hp drat    wt  qsec vs am gear carb
## Mazda RX4         21.0   6  160 110 3.90 2.620 16.46  0  1    4    4
## Mazda RX4 Wag     21.0   6  160 110 3.90 2.875 17.02  0  1    4    4
## Datsun 710        22.8   4  108  93 3.85 2.320 18.61  1  1    4    1
## Hornet 4 Drive    21.4   6  258 110 3.08 3.215 19.44  1  0    3    1
## Hornet Sportabout 18.7   8  360 175 3.15 3.440 17.02  0  0    3    2
## Valiant           18.1   6  225 105 2.76 3.460 20.22  1  0    3    1
```

By just calling the built-in object of mtcars within R, we can see all sorts of columns in the data from which to choose to build a machine learning model. In the machine learning world, columns of data are sometimes also called *features*. Now that we know what we have to work with, we could try seeing if there's a relationship between the car's fuel efficiency and any one of these features, as depicted in Figure 1-2:

```
pairs(mtcars[1:7], lower.panel = NULL)
```

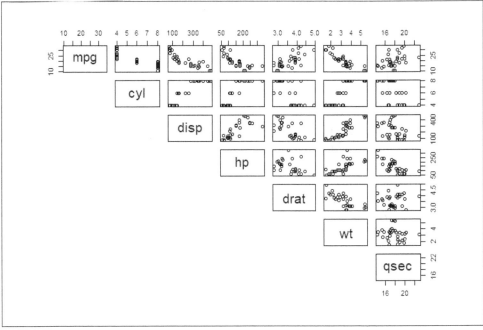

Figure 1-2. A pairs plot of the mtcars dataset, focusing on the first seven rows

Each box is its own separate plot, for which the dependent variable is the text box at the bottom of the column, and the independent variable is the text box at the beginning of the row. Some of these plots are more interesting for trending purposes than others. None of the plots in the cyl row, for example, look like they lend themselves easily to simple regression modeling.

In this example, we are plotting some of those features against others. The columns, or features, of this data are defined as follows:

mpg
   Miles per US gallon

cyl
   Number of cylinders in the car's engine

disp
   The engine's displacement (or volume) in cubic inches

hp
   The engine's horsepower

drat
   The vehicle's rear axle ratio

wt
   The vehicle's weight in thousands of pounds

qsec
   The vehicle's quarter-mile race time

vs
   The vehicle's engine cylinder configuration, where "V" is for a v-shaped engine and "S" is for a straight, inline design

am
   The transmission of the vehicle, where 0 is an automatic transmission and 1 is a manual transmission

gear
   The number of gears in the vehicle's transmission

carb
   The number of carburetors used by the vehicle's engine

You can read the upper-right plot as "mpg as a function of quarter-mile-time," for example. Here we are mostly interested in something that looks like it might have some kind of quantifiable relationship. This is up to the investigator to pick out what patterns look interesting. Note that "mpg as a function of cyl" looks very different from "mpg as a function of wt." In this case, we focus on the latter, as shown in Figure 1-3:

```
plot(y = mtcars$mpg, x = mtcars$wt, xlab = "Vehicle Weight",
    ylab = "Vehicle Fuel Efficiency in Miles per Gallon")
```

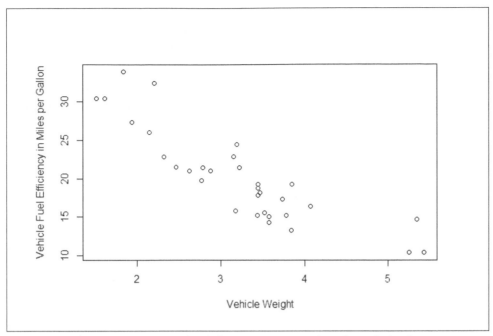

Figure 1-3. This plot is the basis for drawing a regression line through the data

Now we have a more interesting kind of dataset. We still have our fuel efficiency, but now it is plotted against the weight of the respective cars in tons. From this kind of format of the data, we can extract a best fit to all the data points and turn this plot into an equation. We'll cover this in more detail in later chapters, but we use a function in R to model the value we're interested in, called a *response*, against other features in our dataset:

```
mt.model <- lm(formula = mpg ~ wt, data = mtcars)

coef(mt.model)[2]

##          wt
## -5.344472

coef(mt.model)[1]

## (Intercept)
##    37.28513
```

In this code chunk, we modeled the vehicle's fuel efficiency (mpg) as a function of the vehicle's weight (wt) and extracted values from that model object to use in an equation that we can write as follows:

Fuel Efficiency = 5.344 × Vehicle Weight + 37.285

Now if we wanted to know what the fuel efficiency was for any car, not just those in the dataset, all we would need to input is the weight of it, and we get a result. This the benefit of a model. We have predictive power, given some kind of input (e.g., weight), that can give us a value for any number we put in.

The model might have its limitations, but this is one way in which we can help to expand the data beyond a static report into something more flexible and more insightful. A given vehicle's weight might not actually be predictive of the fuel efficiency as given by the preceding equation. There might be some error in the data or the observation.

You might have come across this kind of modeling procedure before in dealing with the world of data. If you have, congratulations—you have been doing machine learning without even knowing it! This particular type of machine learning model is called *linear regression*. It's much simpler than some other machine learning models like neural networks, but the algorithms that make it work are certainly using machine learning principles.

Algorithms Versus Models: What's the Difference?

Machine learning and algorithms can hardly be separated. Algorithms are another subject that can seem impenetrably daunting at first, but they are actually quite simple at their core, and you have probably been using them for a long time without realizing it.

An algorithm is a set of steps performed in order.

That's all an algorithm is. The algorithm for putting on your shoes might be something like putting your toes in the open part of the shoe, and then pressing your foot forward and your heel downward. The set of steps necessary to produce a machine learning algorithm are more complicated than designing an algorithm for putting on your shoes, of course, but one of the goals of this book is to explain the inner workings of the most widely used machine learning models in R by helping to simplify their algorithmic processes.

The simplest algorithm for linear regression involves putting two points on a plot and then drawing a line between them. You get the important parts of the equation (slope and intercept) by taking the difference in the coordinates of those points with respect to some origin. The algorithm becomes more complicated when you try to do the same procedure for more than two points, however. That process involves more equations that can be tedious to compute by hand for a human but very easy for a processor in a computer to handle in microseconds.

A machine learning model like regression or clustering or neural networks relies on the workings of algorithms to help them run in the first place. Algorithms are the engine that underlie the simple R code that we run. They do all the heavy lifting of multiplying matrices, optimizing results, and outputting a number for us to use. There are many types of models in R, which span an entire ecosystem of machine learning more generally. There are three major types of models: regression models, classification models, and mixed models that are a combination of both. We've already encountered a regression model. A classification model is different in that we would be trying to take input data and arrange it according to a type, class, group, or other discrete output. Mixed models might start with a regression model and then use the output from that to help it classify other types of data. The reverse could be true for other mixed models.

The function call for a simple linear regression in R can be written as: `lm(y ~ x)`, or read out loud as "give me the linear model for the variable y as a function of the feature x." What you're not seeing are the algorithms that the code is running to make optimizations based on the data that we give it.

In many cases, the details of these algorithms are beyond the scope of this book, but you can look them up easily. It's very easy to become lost in the weeds of algorithms and statistics when you're simply trying to understand what the difference between a logistic regression machine learning model is compared to a support vector machine model.

Although documentation in R can vary greatly in quality from one machine learning function to the next, in general, one can look up the inner workings of a model by pulling up the help file for it:

```
?(lm)
```

From this help file, you can get a wealth of information on how the function itself works with inputs and what it outputs. Moreover, if you want to know the specific algorithms used in its computation, you might find it here or under the citations listed in the "Author(s)" or "References" sections. Some models might require an extensive digging process to get the exact documentation you are looking for, however.

A Note on Terminology

The word "model" is rather nebulous and difficult to separate from something like a "function" or an "equation." At the beginning of the chapter, we made a report. That was a static object that didn't have any predictive power. We then delved into the data to find another variable that we could use as a modeling input. We used the `lm()` *function* which gave us an equation at the end. We can quickly define these terms as follows:

Report
    A static object with no predictive power.

Function
An object that has some kind of processing power, likely sits inside a model.

Model
A complex object that takes an input parameter and gives an output.

Equation
A mathematical representation of a function. Sometimes a mathematical model.

Algorithm
A set of steps that are passed into a model for calculation or processing.

There are cases in which we use functions that might not yield mathematical results. For example, if we have a lot of data but it's in the wrong form, we might develop a process by which we reshape the data into something more usable. If we were to *model* that process, we could have something more like a flowchart instead of an equation for us to use.

Many times these terms can be used interchangeably, which can be confusing. In some respects, specific terminology is not that important, but knowing that algorithms build into a model *is* important. The lm() code is itself a function, but it's also a linear model. It calls a series of algorithms to find the best values that are then output as a slope and an intercept. We then use those slopes and intercepts to build an equation, which we can use for further analysis.

Modeling Limitations

Statistician George Box is often quoted for the caveat, "All models are wrong, but some are useful." A model is a simplified picture of reality. In reality, systems are complex and ever changing. The human brain is phenomenal at being able to discover patterns and make sense of the universe around us, but even our senses are limited. All models, be they mathematical, computational, or otherwise are limited by the same human brain that designs them.

Here's one classic example of the limits of a model: in the 1700s, Isaac Newton had developed a mathematical formulation describing the motions of objects. It had been well tested and was taken, more or less, to be axiomatic truth. Newton's universal law of gravitation had been used with great success to describe how the planets move around the Sun. However, one outlier wasn't well understood: the orbit of Mercury. As the planet Mercury orbits the Sun, its perihelion (the closest point to the Sun of its orbit) moves around ever so slightly over time. For the longest time, physicists couldn't account for the discrepancy until the early twentieth century when Albert Einstein reformulated the model with his General Theory of Relativity.

Even Einstein's equations break down at a certain level, however. Indeed, when new paradigms are discovered in the world of science, be they from nature throwing us a

Confidence intervals

These are two values between which we expect a parameter to be. For example, a 95% confidence interval between the numbers 1 and 3 might describe where the number 2 sits.

We can use these to understand the difference between a model that fits the data well and one that fits poorly. We can assess which features are useful for us to use in our model and we can determine the accuracy of the answers produced by the model.

The basic mathematical formulation of regression modeling with two data points is something often taught at the middle school level, but rarely does the theory move beyond that to three or more data points. The reason being that to calculate coefficients that way, we need to employ some optimization techniques like *gradient descent*. These are often beyond the scope of middle school mathematics but are an important underpinning of many different models and how they get the most accurate numbers for us to use.

We elaborate on concepts like gradient descent in further detail, but we leave that for the realm of the appendixes. It's possible to run machine learning models without knowing the intricate details of the optimizations behind them, but when you get into more advanced model tuning, or need to hunt for bugs or assess model limitations, it's essential to fully grasp the underpinnings of the tools you are working with.

Data Training

One statistical method that we cover in detail is that of *training data*. Machine learning requires us to first train a data model, but what does that mean exactly? Let's say that we have a model for which we have some input that goes through an algorithm that generates an output. We have data for which we want a prediction, so we pass it through the model and get a result out. We then evaluate the results and see if the associated errors in the model go down or not. If they do, we are tuning the model in the right direction, otherwise if the errors continue to build up, we need to tweak our model further.

It's very important for us to not train our machine learning models on data that we then pass back into it in order to test its validity. If, for example, we train a black box model on 50 data points and then pass those same 50 data points back through the model, the result we get will be suspiciously accurate. This is because our black box example has already seen the data so it basically knows the right answer already.

Often our hands are tied with data availability. We can't pass data we don't have into a model to test it and see how accurate it is. If, however, we took our 50-point dataset and split it in such a way that we used a majority of the data points for training but leave some out for testing, we can solve our problem in a more statistically valid way. The danger with this is splitting into training and test sets when we have only a small number of data points to begin with. But if we were limited in observations to start, using advanced machine learning techniques might not be the best approach anyway.

Now if we have our 50-point dataset and split it so that 80% of our data went into the training set (40 data points) and the rest went into our test set, we can better assess the model's performance. The black box model will be trained on data that's basically the same form as the test set (hopefully), but the black box model hasn't seen the *exact* data points in the test set yet. After the model is tuned and we give it the test set, the model can make some predictions without the problem of being biased as a result of data it has seen before.

Methods of splitting up data for training and testing purposes are known as *sampling techniques.* These can come in many flavors like taking the top 40 rows of data as the training set, taking random rows from our data, or more advanced techniques.

Cross-Validation

Training data is very valuable to tuning machine learning models. Tuning a machine learning model is when you have a bunch of inputs whose values we can change slightly without changing the underlying data. For example, you might have a model that has three parameters that you can tune as follows: A=1, B=2, C="FALSE". If your model doesn't turn out right, you can tweak it by changing the values to A=1.5, B=2.5, C="FALSE", and so forth with various permutations.

Many models have built-in ways to ingest data, perform some operations on it, and then save the tuned operations to a data structure that is used on the test data. In many cases during the training phase, you might want to try other statistical techniques like *cross-validation*. This is sort of like another mini-step of splitting into training and test sets and running the model, but only on the training data. For example, you take your 50-point total dataset and split 80% into a training set, leaving the rest for your final test phase. We are left with 40 rows with which to train your data model. You can split these 40 rows further into a 32-row training set and an 8-row test set. By doing so and going through a similar training and test procedure, you can get an ensemble of errors out of your model and use those to help refine its tuning even further.

Some examples of cross-validation techniques in R include the following:

- Bootstrap cross-validation
- Bootstrap 632 cross-validation
- *k*-fold cross-validation
- Repeated cross-validation
- Leave-one-out cross-validation

- Leave-group-out cross-validation
- Out-of-bag cross-validation
- Adaptive cross-validation
- Adaptive bootstrap cross-validation
- Adaptive leave-group-out cross-validation

We expand on these methods later; their usage is highly dependent on the structure of the data itself. The typical gold standard of cross-validation techniques is *k-fold cross-validation*, wherein you pick $k = 10$ folds against which to validate. This is the best balance between efficient data usage and avoiding splits in the data that might be poor choices. Chapter 3 looks at *k*-fold cross-validation in more detail.

Why Use R?

In this book, we provide a gentle introduction to the world of machine learning as illustrated with code and examples from R. The R language is a free, open source programming language that has its legacy in the world of statistics, being primarily built off of S and subsequently S+. So even though the R language itself has not been around for too long, there is some historical legacy code from its predecessors that have a good syntactic similarity to what we see today. The question is this: why use R in the first place? There are so many programming languages to choose from, how do you know which one is the best for what you want to accomplish?

The Good

R has been growing in popularity at an explosive rate. Complementary tools to learn R have also grown, and there are no shortage of great web-based tutorials and courses to choose from. One package, `swirl`, can even teach you how to use R from within the console itself. Many online courses also do instruction through `swirl` as well. Some cover simple data analysis, others cover more complex topics like mathematical biostatistics.

R also has great tools for accessibility and reproduction of work. Web visualizations like the package `shiny` make it possible for you to build interactive web applications that can be used by non-experts to interact with complex datasets without the need to know or even install R.

There are a number of supported integrated development environments (IDEs) for R, but the most popular one is R Studio, as shown in Figure 1-4.

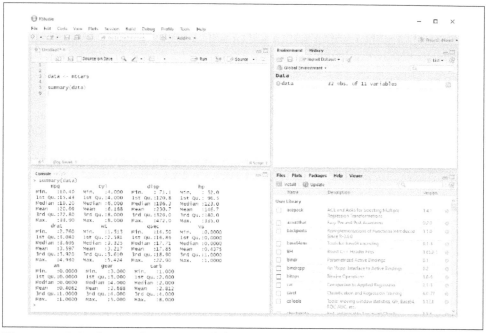

Figure 1-4. R Studio is a free integrated development environment (IDE) for R that is very stable and user-friendly for those new to the language

In fact, this book is being written in R Studio, using R Markdown. R supports a version of Markdown, a lightweight language that you can convert to all sorts of forms for display on the web or rendered to PDF files. It's a great way to share code via publishing on the web or to write professional documentation. Doing so gives you the ability to write large swaths of text but also provide graphical examples such as those shown earlier in the chapter.

Another powerful feature of the language is support for *data frames*. Data frames are like a SQL database in memory that allow you to reshape and manipulate data to summarize and carry out lots of valuable data processing. Unlike a traditional matrix of data in which every column is the same data type, data frames allow you to mix them up. There will be countless times as you work with data when you will have a "Name" field with character data in it, followed by some numerical columns like "ID" or "Sales." Reading that data into some languages can cause a problem if you can't mix and match the data types of the columns.

In the next example, we have three vectors of different types: one numeric, one a vector of factors, and one a vector of logical values. Using data frames, you can combine all of these into a single dataset. More often than not, in the data science world we work with data of mixed types in the same table. Oftentimes, that can be helpful for subsetting the table based on certain criteria for analytical work.

```
v1 = c(1, 2, 3)
v2 = c("Jerry", "George", "Elaine")
v3 = c(TRUE, FALSE, TRUE)

data_frame = data.frame(v1, v2, v3)

str(data_frame)

## 'data.frame':    3 obs. of 3 variables:
## $ v1: num  1 2 3
## $ v2: Factor w/ 3 levels "Elaine","George",..: 3 2 1
## $ v3: logi  TRUE FALSE TRUE
```

Data manipulation takes a majority of the time for those involved in data analysis, and R has several packages to facilitate that work. The dplyr package is a fantastic way to reshape and manipulate data in a verbiage that makes intuitive sense. The lubridate package is a powerful way to do manipulation on tricky datetime-formatted data.

With the dplyr package comes the pipe operator, %>%. This helpful tool allows you to simplify code redundancy. Instead of assigning a variable var1 an input and then using that input in another stage named var2, and so on, you can use this pipe operator as a "then do" part of your code.

R and Machine Learning

R has a lot of good machine learning packages. Some of which you can see on the CRAN home page (*https://cran.r-project.org/web/views/MachineLearning.html*). Yet the list of actual machine learning models is much greater. There are more than 200 types of machine learning models that are reasonably popular in the R ecosystem, and there are fairly strict rules governing each one.

The appendix includes a comprehensive list of more than 200 functions; their package dependencies, if they are used for classification, regression, or both; and any keywords used with them.

We have selected R for this book because machine learning has its basis in statistics, and R is well suited to illustrate those relationships. The ecosystem of statistical modeling packages in R is robust and user-friendly for the most part. Managing data in R is a big part of a data scientist's day-to-day functionality, and R is very well developed for such a task. Although R is robust and relatively easy to learn from a data science perspective, the truth is that there is no single best programming language that will cover all your needs. If you are working on a project that requires the data to be in some specific form, there might be a language that has a package already built for that structure of data to a great degree of accuracy and speed. Other times, you might need to build your own solution from scratch.

R offers a fantastic tool for helping with the modeling process, known as the *function operator*, ~. This symbolic operator acts like an equals sign in a mathematical formula. Earlier we saw the example with a linear model in which we had `lm(mtcars$mpg ~ mtcars$wt)`. In that case, `mtcars$mpg` was our response, the item we want to model as the output, and `mtcars$wt` was the input. Mathematically, this would be like `y = f(x)` in mathematical notation compared with `y ~ x` in R code.

This powerful operator makes it possible for you to utilize multiple inputs very easily. We might expect to encounter a multivariate function in mathematics to be written as follows:

$$y = f(x_1, x_2, x_3, ...)$$

In R, that formulation is very straightforward:

```
y ~ x_1 + x_2 + x_3
```

What we are doing here is saying that our modeling output `y` is not only a function of `x_1`, but many other variables, as well. We will see in dedicated views of machine learning models how we can utilize multiple features or inputs in our models.

The Bad

R has some drawbacks, as well. Many algorithms in its ecosystem are provided by the community or other third parties, so there can be some inconsistency between them and other tools. Each package in R is like its own mini-ecosystem that requires a little bit of understanding first before going all out with it. Some of these packages were developed a long time ago and it's not obvious what the current "killer app" is for a particular machine learning model. You might want to do a simple neural network model, for example, but you also want to visualize it. Sometimes, you might need to select a package you're less familiar with for its specific functionality and leave your favorite one behind.

Sometimes, documentation for more obscure packages can be inconsistent, as well. As referenced earlier, you can pull up the help file or manual page for a given function in R by doing something like `?lm()` or `?rf()`. In a lot of cases, these include helpful examples at the bottom of the page for how to run the function. However, some cases are needlessly complex and can be simplified to a great extent. One goal of this book is to try to present examples in the simplest cases to build an understanding of the model and then expand on the complexity of its workings from there.

Finally, the way R operates from a programmatic standpoint can drive some professional developers up a wall with how it handles things like type casting of data structures. People accustomed to working in a very strict object-oriented language for which you allocate specific amounts of memory for things will find R to be rather lax in its treatment of boundaries like those. It's easy to pick up some bad habits as a result of such pitfalls, but this book aims to steer clear of those in favor of simplicity to explain the machine learning landscape.

Summary

In this chapter we've scoped out the vision for our exploration of machine learning using the R programming language.

First we explored what makes up a model and how that differs from a report. You saw that a static report doesn't tell us much in terms of predictability. You can turn a report into something more like a model by first introducing another feature and examining if there is some kind of relationship in the data. You then fit a simple linear regression model using the lm() function and got an equation as your final result. One feature of R that is quite powerful for developing models is the function operator ~. You can use this function with great effect for symbolically representing the formulas that you are trying to model.

We then explored the semantics of what defines a model. A machine learning model like linear regression utilizes algorithms like gradient descent to do its background optimization procedures. You call linear regression in R by using the lm() function and then extract the coefficients from the model, using those to build your equation.

An important step with machine learning and modeling in general is to understand the limits of the models. Having a robust model of a complex set of data does not prevent the model itself from being limited in scope from a time perspective, like we saw with our mtcars data. Further, all models have some kind of error tied to them. We explore error assessment on a model-by-model basis, given that we can't directly compare some types to others.

Lots of machine learning models utilize complicated statistical algorithms for them to compute what we want. In this book, we cover the basics of these algorithms, but focus more on implementation and interpretation of the code. When statistical concepts become more of a focus than the underlying code for a given chapter, we give special attention to those concepts in the appendixes where appropriate. The statistical techniques that go into how we shape the data for training and testing purposes, however, are discussed in detail. Oftentimes, it is very important to know how to specifically tune the machine learning model of choice, which requires good knowledge of how to handle training sets before passing test data through the fully optimized model.

To cap off this chapter, we make the case for why R is a suitable tool for machine learning. R has its pedigree and history in the field of statistics, which makes it a good platform on which to build modeling frameworks that utilize those statistics. Although some operations in R can be a little different than other programming languages, on the whole R is a relatively simple-to-use interface for a lot of complicated machine learning concepts and functions.

Being an open source programming language, R offers a lot of cutting-edge machine learning models and statistical algorithms. This can be a double-edged sword in terms of help files or manual pages, but this book aims to help simplify some of the more impenetrable examples encountered when looking for help.

In Chapter 2, we explore some of the most popular machine learning models and how we use them in R. Each model is presented in an introductory fashion with some worked examples. We further expand on each subject in a more in-depth dedicated chapter for each topic.

Supervised and Unsupervised Machine Learning

In the universe of machine learning algorithms, there are two major types: *supervised* and *unsupervised*. Supervised learning models are those in which a machine learning model is scored and tuned against some sort of known quantity. The majority of machine learning algorithms are supervised learners. Unsupervised learning models are those in which the machine learning model derives patterns and information from data while determining the known quantity tuning parameter itself. These are more rare in practice, but are useful in their own right and can help guide our thinking on where to explore the data for further analysis.

An example of supervised learning might be something like this: we have a model we've built that says "any business that sells less than 10 units is a *poor* performer, and more than 10 units is a *good* performer." We then have a set of data we want to test against that statement. Suppose that our data includes a store that sells eight units. That is less than 10, so according to our model definition, it is classified as a *poor* performer. In this situation, we have a model that ingests data in which we're interested and gives us an output as decided by the conditions in the model.

In contrast, an unsupervised learning model might be something like this: we have a bunch of data and we want to know how to separate it into meaningful groups. We could have a bunch of data from a survey about people's height and weight. We can use some algorithms in the unsupervised branch to figure out a way to group the data into meaningful clusters for which we might define clothing sizes. In this case, the model doesn't have an answer telling it, "For this person's given height and weight, I should classify them as a small pant size"; it must figure that out for itself.

Supervised Models

Supervised models are more common than their unsupervised counterparts. They come in three major flavors:

Regression
> These models are very common, and it's likely that you encountered one in high school math classes. They are primarily used for looking at how data evolves with respect to another variable (e.g., time) and examining what you can do to predict values in the future.

Classification
> These models are used to organize your data into schemes that make categorical sense. For instance, consider the aforementioned store labeling example—stores that sell more than 10 units per week could be classified as good performers, whereas those selling fewer than that number would be classified as poor.

Mixed
> These models can often rely on parts of regression to inform how to do classification, or sometimes the opposite. One case might be looking at sales data over time and whether there is a rapid change in the slope of the line in some time period.

Regression

Regression modeling is something you most likely have done numerous times without realizing you're doing machine learning. At its core, a regression line is one for which we fit to data that has an x and a y element. We then use an equation to predict what the corresponding output, y, should be for any given input, x. This is always done on numeric data.

Let's take a look at an example regression problem:

```
head(mtcars)
```

```
##                    mpg cyl disp  hp drat    wt  qsec vs am gear carb
## Mazda RX4         21.0   6  160 110 3.90 2.620 16.46  0  1    4    4
## Mazda RX4 Wag     21.0   6  160 110 3.90 2.875 17.02  0  1    4    4
## Datsun 710        22.8   4  108  93 3.85 2.320 18.61  1  1    4    1
## Hornet 4 Drive    21.4   6  258 110 3.08 3.215 19.44  1  0    3    1
## Hornet Sportabout 18.7   8  360 175 3.15 3.440 17.02  0  0    3    2
## Valiant           18.1   6  225 105 2.76 3.460 20.22  1  0    3    1
```

This is one of the many built-in datasets featured in R: the mtcars dataset. It contains data about 32 cars from a 1974 issue of *Motor Trend* magazine. We have 11 features ranging from the car's fuel efficiency in miles per US gallon, to weight, and even whether the car has a manual or automatic transmission. Figure 2-1 plots the fuel efficiency of the cars (mpg) in the dataset as a function of their engine size, or displacement (disp) in cubic inches:

```
plot(y = mtcars$mpg, x = mtcars$disp, xlab = "Engine Size (cubic inches)",
     ylab = "Fuel Efficiency (Miles per Gallon)")
```

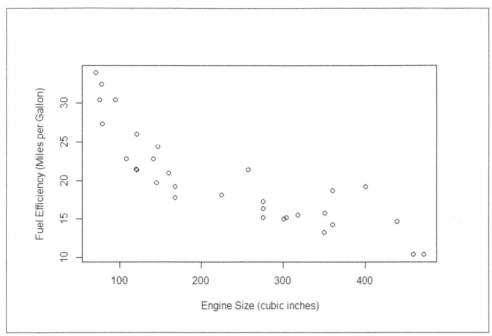

Figure 2-1. A plot of the listed vehicle fuel efficiencies as a function of engine size from the mtcars dataset that comes prepackaged with R

We can see from the plot that the fuel efficiency decreases as the size of the engine increases. However, if you have some new engine for which you want to know the efficiency, the plot in Figure 2-1 doesn't really give you an exact answer. For that, you need to build a linear model:

```
model <- lm(mtcars$mpg ~ mtcars$disp)
coef(model)

## (Intercept) mtcars$disp
## 29.59985476 -0.04121512
```

The cornerstone for regression modeling in R is the lm() function. We are also using another powerful operator featured in R: the formula operator as denoted by ~. You might recall that regression modeling is of the form $y = mx + b$, where the output y is determined from a given slope m, intercept b, and input data x. Your linear model in this case is given by the coefficients that you just computed, so the model looks like the following:

Fuel Efficiency = −0.041 × Engine Size + 29.599

You now have a very simple machine learning model! You can use any input for the engine size and get a value out. Let's look at the fuel efficiency for a car with a 200-cubic-inch displacement:

```
-0.041 * 200 + 25.599
```

```
## [1] 17.399
```

Another, more accurate, way to do this is to call the coefficients from the model directly:

```
coef(model)[2] * 200 + coef(model)[1]
```

```
## mtcars$disp
##    21.35683
```

You can repeat this with any numerical input in which you're interested. Yet you might want to expand this analysis to include other features. You might want a model that computes engine efficiency as a function not only of engine size, but maybe the number of cylinders, horsepower, number of gears, and so on. You might also want to try different functions to fit to the data, because if we try and fit a theoretical engine size of 50,000 cubic inches, the fuel efficiency goes negative! We explore these types of modeling approaches in greater depth in Chapter 4, which focuses exclusively on regression models in R.

Training and Testing of Data

Before we jump into the other major realm of supervised learning, we need to bring up the topic about training and testing data. As we've seen with simple linear regression modeling thus far, we have a model that we can use to predict future values. Yet, we know nothing about how accurate the model is for the moment. One way to determine model accuracy is to look at the R-squared value from the model:

```
summary(model)
```

```
##
## Call:
## lm(formula = mtcars$mpg ~ mtcars$disp)
##
## Residuals:
##     Min      1Q  Median      3Q     Max
## -4.8922 -2.2022 -0.9631  1.6272  7.2305
##
## Coefficients:
##               Estimate Std. Error t value Pr(>|t|)
## (Intercept) 29.599855   1.229720  24.070  < 2e-16 ***
## mtcars$disp -0.041215   0.004712  -8.747 9.38e-10 ***
```

```
## ---
## Signif. codes:  0 '***' 0.001 '**' 0.01 '*' 0.05 '.' 0.1 ' ' 1
##
## Residual standard error: 3.251 on 30 degrees of freedom
## Multiple R-squared:  0.7183, Adjusted R-squared:  0.709
## F-statistic: 76.51 on 1 and 30 DF,  p-value: 9.38e-10
```

The function call `summary()` on our model object gives us a lot of information. The accuracy parameter that's most important to us at the moment is the `Adjusted R-squared` value. This value tells us how linearly correlated the data is; the closer the value is to 1, the more likely the model output is governed by data that's almost exactly a straight line with some kind of slope value to it. The reason we are focusing on the adjusted part instead of the multiple is for future scenarios in which we use more features in a model. For low numbers of features the adjusted and multiple R-squared values are basically the same thing. For models that have many features, we want to use multiple R-squared values, instead, because it will give a more accurate assessment of the model error if we have many dependent features instead of just one.

But what does this tell us as far as an error estimate for the model? We have standard error values from the output, but there's an issue with the model being trained on all the data, then being tested on the same data. What we want to do, in order to ensure an unbiased amount of error, is to split our starting dataset into a training dataset and test dataset.

In the world of statistics, you do this by taking a dataset you have and splitting it into 80% training data and 20% test data. You can tinker with those numbers to your taste, but you always want more training data than test data:

```
split_size = 0.8

sample_size = floor(split_size * nrow(mtcars))

set.seed(123)
train_indices <- sample(seq_len(nrow(mtcars)), size = sample_size)

train <- mtcars[train_indices, ]
test <- mtcars[-train_indices, ]
```

This example sets the split size at 80% and then the sample size for the training set to be 80% of the total number of rows in the `mtcars` data. We then set a seed for reproducibility, then get a list of row indices that we are going to put in our training data. We then split the training and test data by setting the training data to be the rows that contain those indices, and the test data is everything else.

What we want to do now is to build a regression model using only the training data. We then pass the test data values into it to get the model outputs. The key component here is that we have the known data against which we can test the model. That allows us to get a better level of error estimate out:

```
model2 <- lm(mpg ~ disp, data = train)

new.data <- data.frame(disp = test$disp)

test$output <- predict(model2, new.data)

sqrt(sum(test$mpg - test$output)^2/nrow(test))

## [1] 4.627365
```

Let's walk through these steps to calculate the actual error of the model. Before, if you were to look at the residual standard error, you would see a value of 3.521. However, this value is dubious because it was calculated using the same data that was used to train the model. To remedy that, we've split the original mtcars data into a training set that we used exclusively for making the regression model, and a test set which we used to test against.

First, we calculate a new linear model on the training data using lm(). Next, we form a data frame from our test data's disp column. After that, we make predictions on our test set and store that in a new column in our test data. Finally, we compute a root-mean-square error (RMSE) term. We do this by taking the difference between our model output and the known mpg efficiency, squaring it, summing up those squares, and dividing by the total number of entries in the dataset. This gives us the value for the residual standard error. The new value is different from what we've seen before and is an important value for understanding how well our model is performing.

Classification

In contrast to regression modeling, which you have likely previously done without realizing it, classification is a less frequently encountered part of the machine learning spectrum. Instead of predicting continuous values, like numbers, in classification exercises we'll predict discrete values.

Logistic Regression

In contrast to regression, sometimes you want to see if a given data point is of a categorical nature instead of numeric. Before, we were given a numeric input and calculated a numeric output through a simple regression formula. Figure 2-2 presents the same mtcars dataset to visually explain the difference:

```
plot(x = mtcars$mpg, y = mtcars$am, xlab = "Fuel Efficiency (Miles per Gallon)",
     ylab = "Vehicle Transmission Type (0 = Automatic, 1 = Manual)")
```

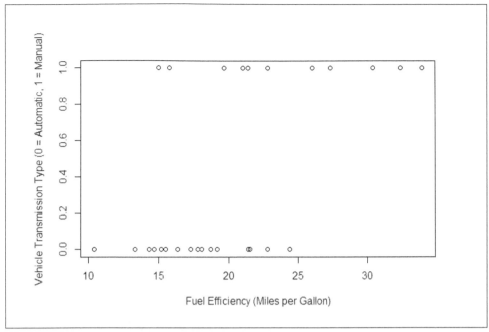

Figure 2-2. This plot of vehicle transmission type as a function of fuel efficiency is very different looking than the plot of efficiency versus engine size

The data looks very different compared to what we saw earlier. In the mtcars dataset, each car is given a 0 or a 1 label to determine whether it has an automatic transmission as defined by the column name am. A car with an automatic has a value 1, whereas a manual transmission car has a value of 0. Fitting a linear regression model to this data would not work, because we cannot have half a transmission value. Instead, we need to rely on a logistic regression model to help classify whether new efficiency data belongs to either the automatic or manual transmission groups.

We have a slightly different question to answer this time: how is the fuel efficiency related to a car's transmission type? We can't rely on the regression modeling procedure here, unfortunately. We could try to fit a regression line to the data, but the results would be very misleading. Instead, we need to use a classification algorithm. In this case, we will use a *logistic regression* algorithm.

Logistic regression is different than linear regression in that we get discrete outputs instead of continuous ones. Before, we could get any number as a result of our regression model, but with our logistic model, we should expect a binary outcome for the transmission type; it either is an automatic transmission, or it isn't. The approach here is different, as well. First, you need to load the caTools library:

```
library(caTools)
```

This library contains many functions, but, most important, it has a function for logistic regression: `LogitBoost`. First, you need to give the model the label against which we want to predict as well as the data that you want to use for training the model:

```
Label.train = train[, 9]
Data.train = train[, -9]
```

You can read the syntax of `train[,-9]` as follows: "The data we want is the `mtcars` dataset that we split into a training set earlier, *except* column number 9." That happens to be the `am` column we used earlier. This is a more compact way of subsetting the data instead of listing out each column individually for input:

```
model = LogitBoost(Data.train, Label.train)
Data.test = test
Lab = predict(model, Data.test, type = "raw")
data.frame(row.names(test), test$mpg, test$am, Lab)
```

```
##        row.names.test. test.mpg test.am        X0           X1
## 1          Datsun 710     22.8       1 0.9820138 0.0179862100
## 2          Merc 450SE     16.4       0 0.9996646 0.0003353501
## 3   Cadillac Fleetwood     10.4       0 0.9996646 0.0003353501
## 4    Chrysler Imperial     14.7       0 0.9996646 0.0003353501
## 5            Fiat 128     32.4       1 0.8807971 0.1192029220
## 6        Toyota Corolla     33.9       1 0.8807971 0.1192029220
## 7        Toyota Corona     21.5       0 0.9820138 0.0179862100
```

Walking through the preceding steps, we first set the label and data by picking the columns that represented each. We got those from the training dataset that we split up earlier. We then passed those into the `LogitBoost` function and made a prediction similar to how we did with a linear regression analysis. The output here is slightly different, though. Here, we have a given engine efficiency in miles per gallon (mpg) and a known value if the car is an automatic transmission (1) or not (0). We then have two columns, `X0` and `X1`, which are probabilities that are output by the model if the car is an automatic transmission (X0) or a manual transmission (X1). Ways to tune this model to be more accurate could include collecting more data in the training dataset, or tuning the options available in the `LogitBoost` function itself.

Supervised Clustering Methods

Clustering is when you have a set of data and want to define classes based on how closely they are grouped. Sometimes, groupings of data might not be immediately obvious, and a clustering algorithm can help you find patterns where they might otherwise be difficult to see explicitly. Clustering is a good example of an ecosystem of algorithms that can be used both in a supervised and unsupervised case. It's one of the most popular forms of classification, and one of the most popular clustering models is the `kmeans` algorithm.

Let's examine the `iris` dataset by looking at the plot of petal width as a function of petal length (Figure 2-3):

```
plot(x = iris$Petal.Length, y = iris$Petal.Width, xlab = "Petal Length",
     ylab = "Petal Width")
```

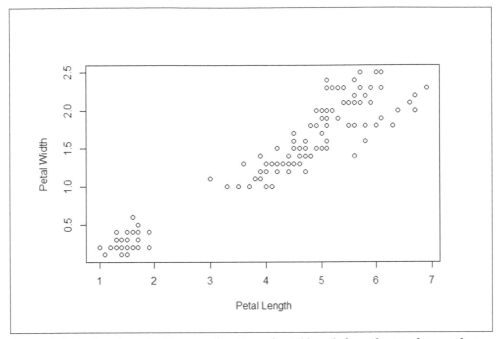

Figure 2-3. A plot of petal width as a function of petal length from the iris dataset that also comes pre-built within R

What if we wanted to try to find three distinct groups in which to classify this dataset? The human brain is remarkably good at finding patterns and structure, so the clumping of data in the lower-left corner of Figure 2-3 stands out as one obvious cluster of data. But what about the rest? How do we go about breaking the data in the upper-right part of the plot into two more groups? One clustering algorithm that can accomplish this is the `kmeans()` approach to clustering.

This algorithm works by first placing a number of random test points in our data—in this case, two. Each of our real data points is measured as a distance from these test points, and then the test points are moved in a way to minimize that distance, as shown in Figure 2-4:

```
data = data.frame(iris$Petal.Length, iris$Petal.Width)

iris.kmeans <- kmeans(data, 2)

plot(x = iris$Petal.Length, y = iris$Petal.Width, pch = iris.kmeans$cluster,
    xlab = "Petal Length", ylab = "Petal Width")
points(iris.kmeans$centers, pch = 8, cex = 2)
```

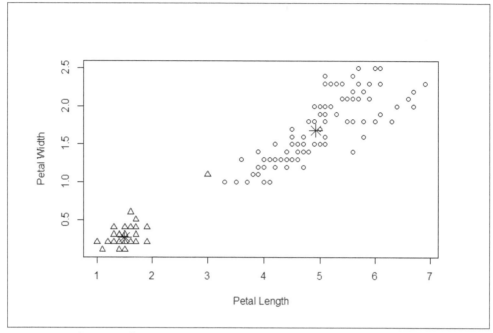

Figure 2-4. The same data as in Figure 2-3, but with the clustering algorithm applied

In Figure 2-4, we can see how the algorithm works by splitting the data into two major groups. In the lower left is one cluster, denoted by the small triangles, and in the upper right there is another cluster labeled with circular data points. We see two big asterisks that mark where the cluster centers have finally stopped iterating. Any point that we further add to the data is marked as being in a cluster if it's closer to one versus another. The points in the lower left are pretty well distinct from the others, but there is one outlier data point. Let's use one more cluster, shown in Figure 2-5, to help make a little more sense of the data:

```
iris.kmeans3 <- kmeans(data, 3)

plot(x = iris$Petal.Length, y = iris$Petal.Width, pch = iris.kmeans3$cluster,
    xlab = "Petal Length", ylab = "Petal Width")

points(iris.kmeans3$centers, pch = 8, cex = 2)
```

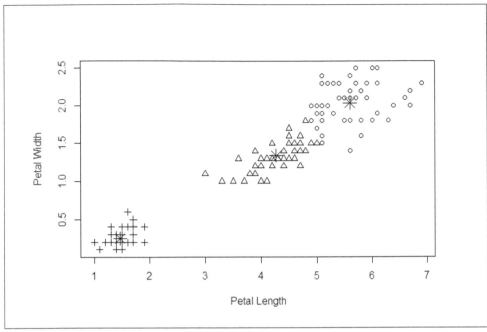

Figure 2-5. By applying another cluster to the data, we can see even more groups by which to classify our dataset

Now you can see that the larger group of data has been split further into two clusters of data that look to be about equal in size. There are three clusters in total with three different centers to the data. You could keep going by adding more and more cluster centers to the data, but you would be losing out on valuable information that way. If every single data point in the set were its own cluster, it would wind up being meaningless as far as classification goes. This is where you need to use a gut intuition to determine the appropriate level of fitting to the data. Too few clusters and the data is underfit: there isn't a good way to determine structure. Too many clusters and you have the opposite problem: there's far too much structure to make sense of simply.

Continuing on the topic of supervised learning, let's take a look at Figure 2-6 and compare this result to the actual answer and see how good our prediction really is:

```
par(mfrow = c(1, 2))

plot(x = iris$Petal.Length, y = iris$Petal.Width, pch = iris.kmeans3$cluster,
    xlab = "Petal Length", ylab = "Petal Width", main = "Model Output")

plot(x = iris$Petal.Length, y = iris$Petal.Width,
    pch = as.integer(iris$Species),
    xlab = "Petal Length", ylab = "Petal Width", main = "Actual Data")
```

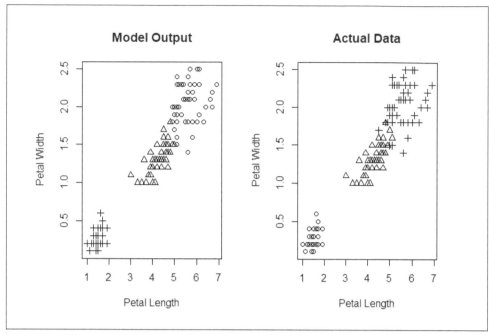

Figure 2-6. Because we have species data against which to test, we can compare our model output, left, with our actual data on the right

Figure 2-6 illustrates how the three-cluster kmeans algorithm works against the actual species labels in the data. It seems to be a fairly good match. We can see the same data represented in tabular format, called a confusion matrix:

```
table(iris.kmeans3$cluster, iris$Species)
```

```
##
##      setosa versicolor virginica
## 1         0          2        46
## 2         0         48         4
## 3        50          0         0
```

You can read this confusion matrix with the output clusters as the rows, and the actual values from the data as the columns. For cluster 1, there are 48 versicolor and six virginica plants. Cluster 2 has only setosa plants, and cluster 3 has two versicolor and 44 virginica plants. If the algorithm were 100% perfect, we would expect each column to have all of its data in one of the three rows that pertain to the clusters, but this isn't a bad result for a cursory example. It shows that there are only six predictions that were off in cluster 1, and two predictions that were off in cluster 3.

Mixed Methods

Thus far, we've discussed regression, which takes in continuous numeric data and then outputs continuous numeric data, and classification, which takes in continuous numeric data and then outputs discrete data, or vice versa. There are many machine learning algorithms in R, and some are focused entirely on regression, whereas others are focused entirely on classification. But there's a third class that can utilize both. Some of these methods can use regression to help inform a classification scheme, or data can be first taken as labels and used to constrain regression models.

Tree-Based Models

So far, we've seen a linear regression and logistic regression example. Part of the universe of machine learning models includes *tree-based* methods. Simply put, a tree is a structure that has nodes and edges. For a decision tree, at each node we might have a value against which we split in order to gain some insight from the data. This is best explained visually by looking at Figure 2-7:

```
library(party)
tree <- ctree(mpg ~ ., data = mtcars)
plot(tree)
```

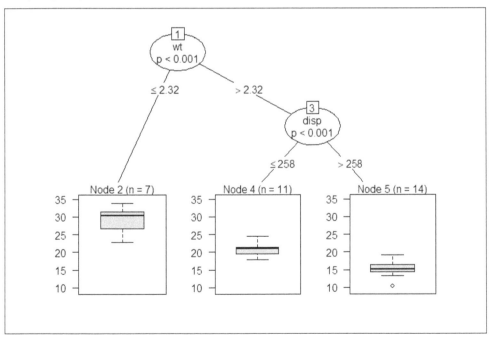

Figure 2-7. An example of a simple decision tree applied to the mtcars dataset

Figure 2-7 demonstrates a plotted conditional inference tree. We are plotting engine fuel efficiency (mpg), but we're using all features in the dataset to build the model instead of just one; hence, the mpg ~ . call in the `ctree()` function. The output is a distribution (in the form of a box-and-whisker plot) of the fuel efficency as a function of the major features that influence it. The `ctree` function calls on certain methods to figure these out; this way, you don't have a bunch of branches in the tree that don't amount to anything other than to clog up the view. In this case, the features that are most important to `mpg` are `disp` (the engine displacement) and `wt` (the car's weight). You read this chart from top to bottom.

At node 1, there is a split for cars that weigh less than 2.32 tons and those that weigh more. For the cars that weigh more, we split further on the engine displacement. For engine displacements that are less than 258 cubic inches in volume, we go to node 4. For engine displacements that have more than 258 cubic inches, we go to node 5. Notice that for each feature there is a statistical *p*-value, which determines how statistically relevant it is. The closer the *p*-value is to 0.05 or greater, the less useful or relevant it is. In this case, a *p*-value of almost exactly 0 is very good. Likewise, you can see how many data points make up each class at the bottom of the tree.

Let's consider a car that has a weight of four tons, and a small engine size of 100 cubic inches. At node 1, we go along the righthand path to node 3 (because the weight is greater than 2.32 tons) and then go left to node 4 based on the theoretical data we just made up. We should expect the fuel efficiency of this car to be somewhere between 13 and 25 miles per gallon.

What if you try to use this new data structure for prediction? The first thing that should pop up is that you are looking at the entire dataset instead of just the training data. Figure 2-8 shows the tree structure for the training data first:

```
tree.train <- ctree(mpg ~ ., data = train)
plot(tree.train)
```

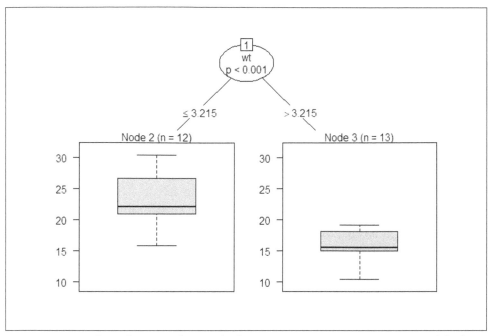

Figure 2-8. By taking the same data and splitting it into a training set, you simplify the picture somewhat. The methodology remains the same for testing purposes, however.

By looking at just the training data, you have a slightly different picture in that the tree depends only on the car's weight. In the following example, there are only two classes instead of the tree as before:

```
test$mpg.tree <- predict(tree.train, test)
test$class <- predict(tree.train, test, type = "node")
data.frame(row.names(test), test$mpg, test$mpg.tree, test$class)

##        row.names.test. test.mpg      mpg test.class
## 1           Datsun 710     22.8 23.46667          2
## 2            Merc 450SE     16.4 16.09231          3
## 3    Cadillac Fleetwood     10.4 16.09231          3
## 4     Chrysler Imperial     14.7 16.09231          3
## 5              Fiat 128     32.4 23.46667          2
## 6        Toyota Corolla     33.9 23.46667          2
## 7         Toyota Corona     21.5 23.46667          2
```

This chunk of code does both a regression and a classification test in two easy lines of code. First, it takes the familiar `predict()` function and applies it to the entirety of the test data and then stores it as a column in the test data. Then, it performs the same procedure, but adds the `type="node"` option to the `predict()` function to get a class out. It then sticks them all together in a single data frame.

What you can see from the end result is that it doesn't take a lot of work for some algorithms to provide both a continuous, numeric output (regression) as well as a discrete class output (classification) for the same input data.

Random Forests

Random forests are a complex topic that we can best approach by using an example about movies. Suppose that you and a friend play a game in which your friend asks you a series of questions to determine whether you would like a movie. Following the logic of the decision tree earlier, you might split on criteria like director, movie run-time, leading actress, and so on. So you might go along the lines of, "Is the movie a comedy?" followed by, "Does Cate Blanchett star in it?" to, "Is it longer than two hours?" This is the basis for how decision trees work, as we've already demonstrated.

Your friend might be able to find a movie you like based on those criteria, but that's just one friend's assessment of your inputs. You want to ask a bunch of your friends, as well. Suppose that you go through the question game again with a few more friends and then they vote if you are interested in a movie. By asking many of your friends instead of just one, you build an *ensemble classifier*, or a forest.

You don't want them to arrive at the same answer by asking the same questions. But you can get insight by asking slightly different questions each time. For example, you tell Amanda that you saw *The Dark Knight* eight times in theaters, but maybe there were reasons why (seen with different friends, scheduling, etc.) that view count could be inflated, so maybe the friends you ask should exclude that example. Maybe you tell Amanda that you cried during the movie *Armageddon*, but only once while cutting an onion, so you should weigh that movie less. Instead of working with the same dataset, you vary it slightly. You aren't changing the end results of liking a movie or not, but you are tinkering with the decisions that led to the result. This is creating a *bootstrapped* version of your beginning data.

So, suppose that Robert suggests *The Rock* because he thinks you like Jerry Bruckheimer movies more than you really do, Max suggests *Kagemusha*, and Will thinks you won't like any of his results and thus recommends nothing. These results are the *aggregated bootstrap forest* of movie preferences. Your friends have now become a random forest.

Random forests aren't as easily describable in model form as a simple $y = mx + b$ equation or a simple tree that has a few nodes in it. You can do the usual training and testing of continuous and discrete data like you have seen with the `ctree()` method, but to illustrate the difference, run the following (Figure 2-9):

```
library(randomForest)

mtcars.rf <- randomForest(mpg ~ ., data = mtcars, ntree = 1000,
    keep.forest = FALSE, importance = FALSE)

plot(mtcars.rf, log = "y", title = "")
```

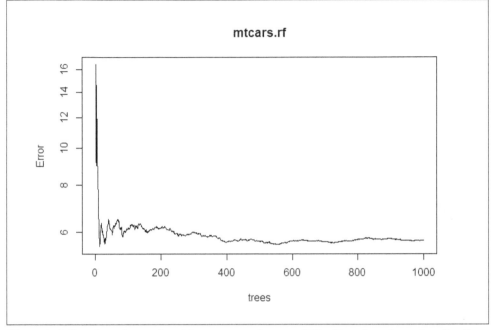

Figure 2-9. Random forest algorithms are much more difficult to show in a visualization; however, we can easily show how the error in the model evolves over the course of how many trees we introduce into the model

Figure 2-9 shows the constraining of error in a random forest algorithm with 1,000 trees used. This is as if you had 1,000 friends playing the movie guessing game for recommendations. You can see that the error goes down with the more trees that you use, and is minimal at around the n=500 trees area.

Neural Networks

A *neural network*, as its name implies, takes its computational form from the way neurons in a biological system work. In essence, for a given list of inputs, a neural network performs a number of processing steps before returning an output. The complexity in neural networks comes in how many of the processing steps there are, and how complex each particular step might be.

A very simple example of how a neural network can work is through the use of *logic gates*. We use logical functions often in programming, but just as a refresher, an AND function is only true if both inputs are true. If one or both inputs are false, the result is false:

```
TRUE & TRUE

## [1] TRUE

TRUE & FALSE

## [1] FALSE

FALSE & FALSE

## [1] FALSE
```

We can define a simple neural network as one that takes in two inputs, calculates the AND function, and gives us a result. These can be represented in graphical form where you have layers and nodes. Layers are vertical sections of the visual, and nodes are the points of computation within each layer. The mathematics of this requires the use of a *bias variable*, which is just a constant we add to the equation for calculation purposes and is represented as its own node, typically at the top of each layer in the neural network.

In the case of the AND function, we'll use numeric values passed into a classification function to give a value of 1 for TRUE and 0 for FALSE. We can do this using the sigmoid function:

$$f(x) = \frac{1}{1 + e^{-x}}$$

So, for negative values of x that are less than –5, the function is basically 0. For positive values of x greater than 5, the function is basically 1. If we had a predefined set of weights for each node in the neural network, we could have a picture that looks like Figure 2-10.

We start with the inputs X1, X2, and the bias node which is just an additive constant. We calculate all of these at the empty circle, which signifies a computation node. The computation that we perform is putting all these things into an activation function, which is almost always a sigmoid function. The output of the sigmoid function is the result of the neural network! Cool, huh?

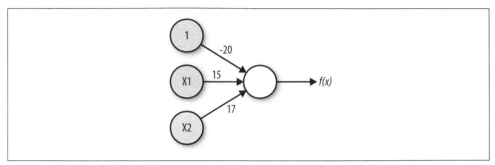

Figure 2-10. An example neural network represented in a diagram read from left to right

Lets walk through this slowly. To calculate the end result of an AND gate (the $f(x)$ on the right side of Figure 2-10), we need to take in inputs for x_1 and x_2. We are defining TRUE to be 1 and FALSE to be 0. The last input we have is the bias variable, which is 1 in this simple case. When the network is trained, we will find weights that are tied to each input. We then build an equation using those weights and find out what that equation's result is. We then pass that result through a sigmoid function (the empty circle) and get the answer out the other side.

This might seem a little overwhelming at first, but we can explain it rather simply mathematically. The weights we have are: $-20 + 15 * x_1 + 17 * x_2$. If x_1 is TRUE, it's a 1, otherwise a 0. We then solve the equation and pass the final value through the sigmoid. We repeat this for all combinations of our input variables:

$x_1 = 1, x_2 = 1$
$h(x) = f(-20 + 15 + 17)$
$h(x) = f(12) \approx 1$

$x_1 = 1, x_2 = 0$
$h(x) = f(-20 + 15)$
$h(x) = f(-5) \approx 0$

$x_1 = 0, x_2 = 1$
$h(x) = f(-20 + 17)$
$h(x) = f(-3) \approx 0$

$x_1 = 0, x_2 = 0$
$h(x) = f(-20) \approx 0$

To recap, we started with a single layer of variables that have some predefined weight tied to them. We passed that into a processing layer, in this case a sigmoid function, and got a result out. At its very basic level, this is a neural network. However, they can become much more complicated if there are multiple processing layers or steps, or more variables to compute. For example, if we wanted to pipe the result of our AND function into an OR function and then into an XOR function, the neural network would become quite cumbersome to describe visually.

We have a number of aspects in a neural network to be cognizant of:

The input layer
> This is a layer that takes in a number of features, including a bias node, which is often just an offset parameter.

The hidden layer, or "compute" layer
> This is the layer that computes some function of each feature. The number of nodes in this hidden layer depends on the computation. Sometimes, it might be as simple as one node in this layer. Other times, the picture might be more complex with multiple hidden layers.

The output layer
> This is a final processing node, which might be a single function.

This code example uses the `iris` dataset that is also built in with R:

```
set.seed(123)
library(nnet)
iris.nn <- nnet(Species ~ ., data = iris, size = 2)

## # weights:  19
## initial  value 209.022391
## iter  10 value 96.222855
## iter  20 value 14.106580
## iter  30 value 6.033138
## iter  40 value 5.981137
## iter  50 value 5.978256
## iter  60 value 5.971562
## iter  70 value 5.967520
## iter  80 value 5.965048
## iter  90 value 5.962782
## iter 100 value 5.960028
## final  value 5.960028
## stopped after 100 iterations
```

This code uses the `nnet()` function with the familiar operator that we've been using with our previous examples. The `size=2` option tells us that we are using two hidden layers for computation, which must be explicitly specified. The output that we see are iterations of the network.

After the neural network has finally converged, we can use it for prediction:

```
table(iris$Species, predict(iris.nn, iris, type = "class"))

##
##              setosa versicolor virginica
##   setosa         50          0         0
##   versicolor      0         49         1
##   virginica       0          1        49
```

The result in the confusion matrix are the reference iris species of flowers across the top and the predicted iris species of flowers going up and down the table. So, we see the neural network performed perfectly for classifying the data of the setosa species, but missed one classification for the versicolor and virginica species, respectively. A perfect machine learning model would have zeroes for all the off-diagonal elements, but this is pretty good for an illustrative example.

Support Vector Machines

Support vector machines, or SVMs, are another algorithm that you can use for both regression and classification. Oftentimes, it is introduced as a simpler or faster corollary to a neural network. SVMs work in a manner that's similar in many respects to logistic regression. There are more statistical complexities around SVMs that we explore in greater detail in Chapter 7, but the idea is that we are taking data and trying to find a plane or a line that can separate the data into different classes, as demonstrated in Figure 2-11.

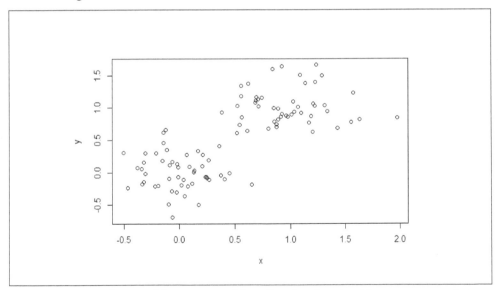

Figure 2-11. Two classes of data separated by a line (or plane), with some vectors that describe a margin or buffer zone between the points being separated and the plane separating them

Suppose that you have *n* features in your data and *m* observations, or rows. If *n* is much greater than *m* (e.g., $n = 1,000$, $m = 10$), you would want to use a logistic regressor. If you have the opposite (e.g., $n = 10$, $m = 1,000$), you might want to use an SVM instead.

Alternatively, you can use a neural network for either case, but it might be considerably slower to train than one of these specific algorithms.

You can do SVM classification in a very similar manner to neural network classification, like we saw previously:

```
library(e1071)
iris.svm <- svm(Species ~ ., data = iris)
table(iris$Species, predict(iris.svm, iris, type = "class"))
```

```
##
##            setosa versicolor virginica
##   setosa       50          0         0
##   versicolor    0         48         2
##   virginica     0          2        48
```

The results here for SVM classification look to be very similar to the `nnet()` function's results. The only difference here is that the predicted number of versicolor species of flowers differed by one compared to our `nnet()` classifier.

Previously, we laid out a basic view of a particular type of neural network. Although the underlying idea behind SVMs and neural networks might be different at the surface level, these two algorithms compete with each other for dominance relatively frequently. One criticism of neural networks is that they can be computationally expensive at scale or slow depending on the complexity of the calculation. SVMs can be quicker in some cases. On the flip side, deep neural networks can represent more "intelligent" functions compared to the simpler SVM architecture.[1] Neural networks can handle multiple inputs, wheras SVMs can handle only one at a time.

Unsupervised Learning

So far, with supervised learning algorithms, we've taken a set of data, broken it into a training and a test set, trained the model, and then evaluated its performance with the test data. Unsupervised learning algorithms take a different approach in that they try to define the overall structure of the data. In principle, these won't have a test set against which to evaluate the model's performance.

---

1 Bengio, Yoshua, and Yann LeCun. *Scaling Learning Algorithms Towards Ai* (*http://yann.lecun.com/exdb/ publis/pdf/bengio-lecun-07.pdf*). 2007.

Generally, most machine learning models you'll encounter will be supervised learning approaches. You build a model, train and test the data, and then compare the outputs to some known parameters. Unsupervised learning doesn't have any "answer" value against which we compare to score the model. Model evaluation and scoring is done in a slightly different manner in this regard. One example of which can be text mining. An unsupervised learner modeled on text from all of Abraham Lincoln's writings might be used to try to build an artificial intelligence (AI) that would write documents like he would author, based on word frequency and proximity to other words. Implicitly, there's no immediate "right" answer against which you would evaluate your Abraham Lincoln bot. Instead, you would need to score that case by what kind of contextual sense the model would generate.

The most common form of unsupervised learning is clustering. We've seen clustering in action already, masked in an example of supervised learning. We were able to run with that example because we had an answer key to use for comparison. But what if we didn't have some data for which we knew the answer?

Unsupervised Clustering Methods

In this unsupervised version of clustering, you are going to take data that has no explicit categorical label and try to categorize them yourself. If you generate some random data, you don't really know how it will cluster up. As Figure 2-12 illustrates, you can perform the usual `kmeans` clustering algorithm here to see how the data should be classified:

```
x <- rbind(matrix(rnorm(100, sd = 0.3), ncol = 2), matrix(rnorm(100,
    mean = 1, sd = 0.3), ncol = 2))

colnames(x) <- c("x", "y")


plot(x)
```

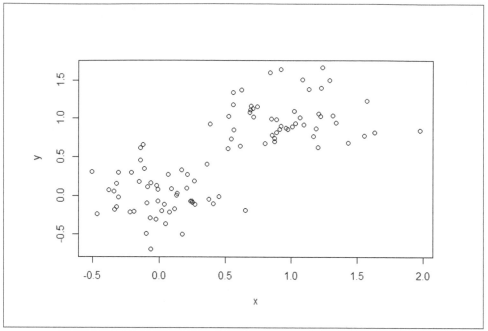

Figure 2-12. A random distribution of data that we want to classify into two distinct clusters; cases like these are difficult to figure out with the naked eye, but unsupervised methods like kmeans can help

What we've done here is generate a random set of data that is normally distributed into two groups. In this case, it might be a little tougher to see where the exact groupings are, but luckily, as Figure 2-13 illustrates, the kmeans algorithm can help designate which points belong to which group:

```
cl <- kmeans(x, 2)

plot(x, pch = cl$cluster)
```

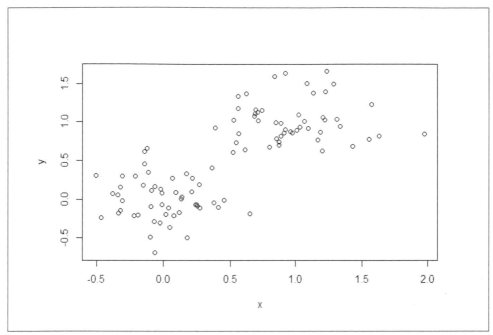

Figure 2-13. Randomly distributed data points with clustering classification labels applied

However, because the dataset has no explicit label tagged to it prior to applying the `kmeans` classification, the best you can do is to label future data points according to the clustering centers. You can see those by printing them out from the `cl` variable:

```
cl[2]
```

```
## $centers
##             x           y
## 1 -0.002450337 0.009187754
## 2  0.975466213 1.014152268
```

Row 1 denotes the x,y coordinates of the first cluster, and likewise for row 2. Any point that you add to the dataset that is closer to either of these cluster centers will be labeled accordingly.

Summary

In this chapter, we explored a series of machine learning algorithms in R that cover both supervised and unsupervised cases. A machine learning algorithm is supervised when there is a test set against which you can evaluate the algorithm's performance. You do this by taking what data you do have, splitting it into a training set that comprises 80% of the total data, and then save the rest for the test set. You train the machine learning algorithm on the training set and then pass the test set through the trained model. You can then evaluate the model's performance on the test set with the known values. That way, when you get new data to evaluate, you can know the limits of the machine learning model's accuracy.

We also took some cursory glances at the difference between regression (continuous data in, continuous data out), and classification (discrete data in, discrete data out). There are many machine learning algorithms that you can use for both, details of which we explore at a finer level in each algorithm's corresponding chapter.

For supervised learning, we covered the most popular algorithms and how to implement them at a very basic level:

- Linear regression, `lm()`, for defining a simple equation by which you can describe a relationship between an output and a number of features attributed to it
- Logistic regression, `LogitBoost()`, for determining a way to separate numeric data into classes
- *k*-means clustering, `kmeans()`, for developing clusters and labeling data according to how those clusters evolve
- Conditional inference trees, `ctree()`, for defining splits in data and performing regressions or classifications on the split data
- Random forests, `randomForest()`, for a more in-depth and accurate, yet less intuitive solution than conditional inference trees
- Support vector machines, `svm()`, for when you might have fewer features than observations and aren't getting good results from logistic regression

In the upcoming chapters, we dive into specific machine learning models in R and how best to apply them. We cover the most popular algorithms used for each model and what caveats to be wary of. Although we are thorough with our statistical underpinnings of the algorithms themselves, we touch on those specifics briefly in each dedicated chapter, leaving the chapter itself mostly for code examples. Statistical derivations are provided in appropriate appendixes.

## CHAPTER 3

Sampling Statistics and Model Training in R

Sampling and machine learning go hand in hand. In machine learning, we typically begin with a big dataset that we want to use for predicting something. We usually split this data into a training set and build a model around that, and then unleash a fully trained model on some kind of test set to see what the final output is. In some instances, it might be very difficult to run a machine learning model on an entire dataset, whereas we might achieve as good an accuracy by running on a small sample of it and testing when appropriate. This could be due to the size of the data, for example.

First let's define some statistical terms. A *population* is the entire collection (or universe) of things under consideration. A *sample* is a portion of the population that we select for analysis. So, for example, we could start with a full dataset, break off a chunk into a sample, and do our training there. Another way to look at it is that some data that we're given to start with might itself be only a sample of a much broader dataset.

Polling data is an example of sampling, and is typically gathered by asking questions of people for specific demographics. By design, the polling data can be only a subset of the general population of a country, because it would be quite an achievement to ask everyone in a country what their favorite color might be. If we have a country with a population of 100 million and we conduct a poll that has 30 million respondents, we've performed a kind of sampling. To fully understand what everyone in the country's favorite color is, we need to do some extrapolation from the sample to the population to paint the full picture.

In the world of statistical science, we have values associated with the total population (i.e., the country level) and those associated with smaller samples of that population, as shown in Figure 3-1.

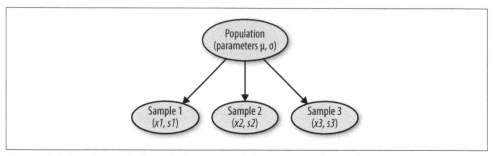

Figure 3-1. Mathematical symbols used to define statistical sampling techniques

When we talk about values related to the terms *mean, variance,* and *standard deviation* in relation to the total population, these are called *parameters*. When we talk about those same values, but specific to a certain subset of the data, we call them *statistics*. So, we might be looking at a specific subset of a country and look at the *mean statistic* in that case, comparing it to the *mean parameter* of the total population. For example, the number of people in a country whose favorite color is blue would be the parameter, and the number of people in a particular city whose favorite color is blue would be the statistic. These values can be different between the population and the samples, but they can also vary between samples, as well.

Bias

Sampling bias is what happens when you sample data in such a way that distributions of data in the samples don't match up with the distributions of the population from which you are drawing. Suppose that you poll a country and the northern half's favorite color is yellow and the southern half's favorite color is green. If you were to do a poll that drew only from people in the southern half of the country, you would have a favorite color distribution that is entirely yellow, and vice versa. Your sample would be biased heavily one way or the other. Sample variation is the extent to which a sample statistic (maybe favorite food as opposed to color) differs from the population. Both of these can be controlled by picking the right way of sampling our data.

Bias and variance with sampling can be represented in four ways. Figure 3-2 shows four bull's-eye targets, with the center of each one being the population mean. The blue dots could represent different polls we run (different samples):

Low bias, low variance
    The best-case scenario. Samples are pretty well representative of the population.

High bias, low variance
    The samples are all pretty consistent, but not really reflective of the population.

Low bias, high variance

   The samples vary wildly in their consistency, but some might be representative of the population.

High bias, high variance

   The samples are a little more consistent, but not likely to be representative of the population.

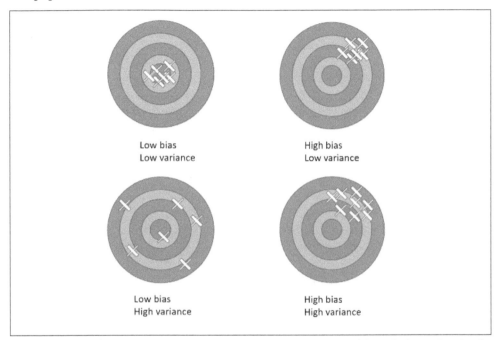

Figure 3-2. When taking samples of data, you need to be wary of four different levels of bias and variance that you could have

A simple *random sample* is one way of controlling bias when pulling samples from a population statement.[1] This is when you select values from your data at random such that every row has an equal chance of being selected, as depicted in Figure 3-3. This is often the best balance of simplicity and representation of the population overall. Applying a simple random sample to the same data twice will have the possibility of selecting the same data, if it's truly random.

---

1 Schaeaffer, R., W. Mendenhall, et al. *Elementary Survey Sampling*, 3rd Ed. Boston: PSW-Kent, 1986.

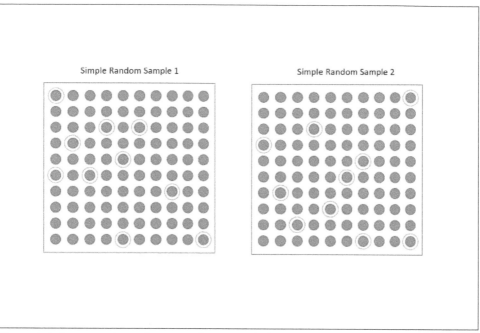

Figure 3-3. In a simple random sample, you pick data points that you want to use from the population by selecting them randomly

Another common form of sampling is called *stratified random sampling* (or oversampling). This is when you separate the data into mutually exclusive groups, called *strata*, and then do a simple random sample on each stratum, as demonstrated in Figure 3-4. This would be like polling randomly across each country's state. This has two advantages over a simple random sample:

- It ensures representation in each strata.
- It can be more accurate than a simple random sample if there is more variation in one strata than others.

If, for example, the samples were spread out geographically or spatially, you could perform a *cluster sample*; for example, when you have data that is stratified by country or city. This is similar to us performing a stratified random sample, but picking the entire strata randomly instead of doing a simple random sample within the strata, as illustrated in Figure 3-5.

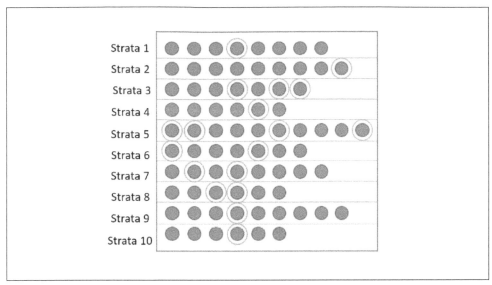

Figure 3-4. A stratified random sample is when you randomly select from various strata in your data (a strata could be a grouping or cut in the data that separates one part of it from another—this could be due to classification or factor variables in the data, too)

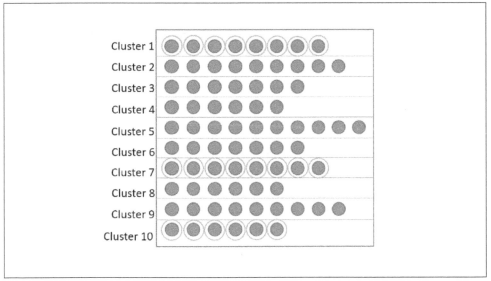

Figure 3-5. Cluster sampling is when you take all of the data points from a given class or cut in the data, where the classes or cuts themselves are randomly selected

A *systematic sample* (Figure 3-6) is when you randomly select from your first *n* data points, and then select every *n*th data point thereafter. This isn't random, per se (other than the initial randomization to find the seed on which to iterate), but it's easy to perform on databases.

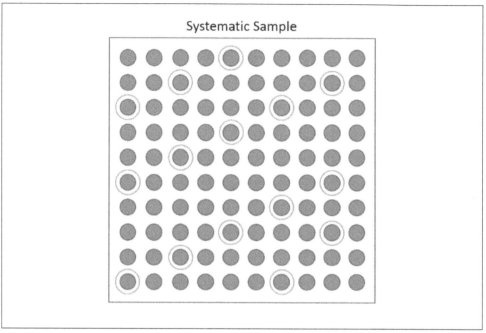

Figure 3-6. With a systematic sampling procedure, you randomly pick a number, n, and then pick every nth data point in the dataset

Thus far we've covered four different types of sampling: simple random sampling, stratified random sampling, cluster sampling, and systematic sampling. In almost all cases, you will use a simple random sample for speed and ease of implementation. However, certain cases might require you to stratify the data first before sampling. Or, if the data is arranged in such a way like being distributed over geographical regions, you might prefer to use a cluster method, instead.

All of this so far talks about implementation but says nothing about how big of a sample you should be taking. The answer here, invariably, is "it depends." As you'll see in coming sections, taking 100% of the population as your sample isn't always the best approach. However, you do need to strike a balance such that your sample has enough data points to be statistically significant and well-representative of the population statistics you're looking at.

Sampling in R

It's quite easy to perform all the aforementioned sampling techniques in R. If we start with some example data—for example, the `iris` dataset—we can test some of these sampling techniques using R code:

```
iris.df <- data.frame(iris)

sample.index <- sample(1:nrow(iris.df), nrow(iris) * 0.75, replace = FALSE)
head(iris[sample.index, ])
```

```
##     Sepal.Length Sepal.Width Petal.Length Petal.Width    Species
## 117          6.5         3.0          5.5         1.8  virginica
## 119          7.7         2.6          6.9         2.3  virginica
## 35           4.9         3.1          1.5         0.2     setosa
## 81           5.5         2.4          3.8         1.1 versicolor
## 53           6.9         3.1          4.9         1.5 versicolor
## 10           4.9         3.1          1.5         0.1     setosa
```

This code chunk does a simple random sample of the `iris` dataset by first generating the indices by which you need to subset your `iris` data. In this case, we randomly selected five rows of data without replacement. Replacement is the option by which, if enabled, when you randomly draw out a row from your data, you have the chance of drawing that same row again. By default, this option is turned off in the `sample()` function in R, as is the case with most sampling functions you see in the programming world.

Let's see how to do stratified sampling in R. In contrast to the simple random sample, stratified sampling can be performed over differing features in the dataset. Let's expand on this by looking at the distributions of data in the `iris` dataset:

```
summary(iris)
```

```
##   Sepal.Length    Sepal.Width     Petal.Length    Petal.Width
## Min.   :4.300   Min.   :2.000   Min.   :1.000   Min.   :0.100
## 1st Qu.:5.100   1st Qu.:2.800   1st Qu.:1.600   1st Qu.:0.300
## Median :5.800   Median :3.000   Median :4.350   Median :1.300
## Mean   :5.843   Mean   :3.057   Mean   :3.758   Mean   :1.199
## 3rd Qu.:6.400   3rd Qu.:3.300   3rd Qu.:5.100   3rd Qu.:1.800
## Max.   :7.900   Max.   :4.400   Max.   :6.900   Max.   :2.500
##          Species
## setosa    :50
## versicolor:50
## virginica :50
##
##
##
```

Here, you can see the population of the data. We intend to get a sample that has roughly the same distribution of values for any of these features. Note that some of these columns vary to a higher degree than others. In this case, `Petal.Length` has the highest amount of variance, followed by `Sepal.Length`. Keep this in mind for the stratified sampling exercise, but for now let's do a simple random sample on just the `Sepal.Length` values:

```
summary(iris[sample.index, ])
```

```
##   Sepal.Length    Sepal.Width     Petal.Length    Petal.Width
## Min.   :4.40    Min.   :2.000   Min.   :1.200   Min.   :0.100
## 1st Qu.:5.10    1st Qu.:2.800   1st Qu.:1.500   1st Qu.:0.275
## Median :5.70    Median :3.000   Median :4.250   Median :1.300
## Mean   :5.82    Mean   :3.067   Mean   :3.694   Mean   :1.164
## 3rd Qu.:6.40    3rd Qu.:3.400   3rd Qu.:5.100   3rd Qu.:1.800
## Max.   :7.90    Max.   :4.400   Max.   :6.900   Max.   :2.500
##         Species
## setosa    :40
## versicolor:35
## virginica :37
##
##
##
```

This example takes a 75% sample of the original data, and you can see that the distributions are all pretty close to what the main population values are. Now let's try the stratified sampling. For this, you need the `fifer` package and the `stratified()` function from it:

```
library(fifer)
```

```
## Loading required package: MASS
```

```
summary(stratified(iris, "Sepal.Length", 0.7))
```

```
##   Sepal.Length    Sepal.Width     Petal.Length    Petal.Width
## Min.   :4.300   Min.   :2.000   Min.   :1.100   Min.   :0.100
## 1st Qu.:5.100   1st Qu.:2.775   1st Qu.:1.500   1st Qu.:0.300
## Median :5.800   Median :3.000   Median :4.350   Median :1.300
## Mean   :5.867   Mean   :3.046   Mean   :3.775   Mean   :1.187
## 3rd Qu.:6.425   3rd Qu.:3.325   3rd Qu.:5.100   3rd Qu.:1.800
## Max.   :7.900   Max.   :4.400   Max.   :6.900   Max.   :2.500
##         Species
## setosa    :35
## versicolor:39
## virginica :34
##
##
##
```

The stratified sample has just about the same values. We performed stratified sampling on the `iris` data using the `stratified()` function, specifically focusing on the strata of `Sepal.Length`. The code then asks for a 70% sample.

With stratified sampling, though, you can specify which particular strata that you want to sample over. If you are sampling over many strata, you generally want to start with the features that vary the least and then work your way upward. The features with the lowest variance in the `iris` dataset are `Sepal.Width` and `Petal.Width`, so let's start with those:

```
summary(stratified(iris, c("Sepal.Width", "Petal.Width"), 0.7))
```

```
##   Sepal.Length    Sepal.Width     Petal.Length    Petal.Width
## Min.   :4.30   Min.   :2.000   Min.   :1.100   Min.   :0.10
## 1st Qu.:5.10   1st Qu.:2.800   1st Qu.:1.575   1st Qu.:0.30
## Median :5.80   Median :3.000   Median :4.250   Median :1.30
## Mean   :5.86   Mean   :3.055   Mean   :3.791   Mean   :1.22
## 3rd Qu.:6.40   3rd Qu.:3.300   3rd Qu.:5.100   3rd Qu.:1.80
## Max.   :7.90   Max.   :4.400   Max.   :6.900   Max.   :2.50
##         Species
## setosa    :37
## versicolor:39
## virginica :40
##
##
##
```

You can see from the output that the stratified sampling with multiple groups still has a good representation of the population data (i.e., the full `iris` dataset) that you started with. The means and the variances all look pretty appropriate for a sample.

For systematic sampling, you can write a simple function that selects every *n*th row sequentially given some random initialization number:

```
sys.sample = function(N, n) {
    k = ceiling(N/n)
    r = sample(1:k, 1)
    sys.samp = seq(r, r + k * (n - 1), k)
}
```

```
systematic.index <- sys.sample(nrow(iris), nrow(iris) * 0.75)
summary(iris[systematic.index, ])
```

```
##   Sepal.Length     Sepal.Width     Petal.Length    Petal.Width
## Min.   :4.300   Min.   :2.200   Min.   :1.10   Min.   :0.10
## 1st Qu.:5.100   1st Qu.:2.800   1st Qu.:1.55   1st Qu.:0.35
## Median :5.700   Median :3.000   Median :4.20   Median :1.30
## Mean   :5.847   Mean   :3.051   Mean   :3.74   Mean   :1.18
## 3rd Qu.:6.400   3rd Qu.:3.250   3rd Qu.:5.10   3rd Qu.:1.80
## Max.   :7.900   Max.   :4.400   Max.   :6.70   Max.   :2.50
## NA's   :37      NA's   :37      NA's   :37     NA's   :37
##         Species
## setosa    :25
## versicolor:25
## virginica :25
## NA's      :37
```

```
##
##
##
```

This code chunk defines the systematic sampling function and then runs that on the `iris` data. For this example, we ran it by giving the number of rows so we could get specified indices against which to subset, but the results look pretty similar to what you've seen thus far.

Training and Testing

When building a predictive model, you need to go through phases of validation to ensure that you can trust its results. If you build a model, you need a verifiable way of making sure that you're getting something that looks like the right answer first before you go crazy and start putting it into production. You need a way to see what the errors generated by the model will be so that you can better tune it appropriately, as well.

For example, if you want to predict the value for some stock price tomorrow for which it's impossible to get the data, you could build a model that is trained on data from a few days ago and test it on data that you have from yesterday. Because you already have the answers for stock prices from yesterday, seeing what the model outputs and comparing the numbers can provide valuable feedback to see whether the model is working.

You might have seen machine learning models using a train-and-test methodology. This is when you take some data, sample a majority of it into a training set, and keep what's left over for a test set. We typically do a 70/30 split of the data into the training/ test subsets, but it's not uncommon to see 80/20 splits, as well. What you accomplish by doing this is to effectively simulate the model working by first running it on data that you already have, before throwing completely new data at it. There are two major assumptions that we work with when doing these training/test splits:

- The data is a fair representation of the actual processes that you want to model (i.e., the subset accurately reflects the population).
- The processes that you want to model are relatively stable over time and that a model built with last month's data should accurately reflect next month's data.

If your assumptions are correct, a model built on today's (or yesterday's) data, should work on any future data you pass through it. You should be careful about the way you split your training and test data, though. The first part of this chapter details different ways for you to sample and subset your starting data in ways that preserve the overall distributions of the features in the data. We definitely don't want to subset our starting data into a subset that has all of one flower type or all of one city's responses to a favorite color poll, for example.

Roles of Training and Test Sets

When you split the data into a training and test set, it's the training set that that you use for model training. Almost all unsupervised learning algorithms follow this format. The specific coefficients you get as a result of the modeling procedures are entirely based on the training dataset and don't depend at all on the test data.

The role of the training set of data is to provide a platform upon which the model of your choice goes about its mathematical way of determining coefficients or whatever it might do under the hood. The role of the test set of data is to see how well that model stacks up against real data.

Why Make a Test Set?

There are two ways to think about the value of making a test set of your data for modeling purposes. The first is just a solid way of validating that data. If you had a model that worked really well for all of the data it was trained on, but crashed and burned when any new data was introduced to it, the model loses all of its predictive power and isn't any better than a static report. At worst, it can be very misleading about how you should think about values in the future! So being able to see that the model performs poorly ahead of time is valuable in and of itself. That insight can inform you that you just need to tweak parameter X by a small amount to fit it, for example.

The other valuable need for a test set is that some machine learning algorithms actually depend on one to exist in the first place. For example, classification and regression trees (CARTs) can be so flexible in their modeling capabilities that, if the tree is large enough, you can often get misleading predictions. You might train a CART model and see that the output is 100% accurate. In reality, the model will perform poorly on any new data it sees. From a statistical standpoint, any model that gives you 100.0% accuracy should be cause for concern. You can use the test set to evaluate the predictive performance of the trees in the data to find the one with the lowest error. Thus, the test set acts not only as a way to validate the data, but as a way to select which form of the model you need, depending on the algorithm in play.

Training and Test Sets: Regression Modeling

We can best illustrate the need for train/test splits of your data by working through some simple regression examples. Let's begin with some sample data (Figure 3-7):

```
set.seed(123)

x <- rnorm(100, 2, 1)
```

```
y = exp(x) + rnorm(5, 0, 2)

plot(x, y)

linear <- lm(y ~ x)

abline(a = coef(linear[1], b = coef(linear[2], lty = 2)))
```

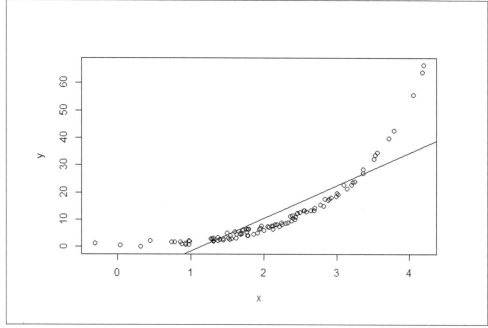

Figure 3-7. Randomized data with a linear fit attached; the linear fit comes close to fitting some data points, but not all (the further you extend X out, the more likely it is that your linear fit won't approximate the data very well)

The following output is the result of the code prior to Figure 3-7:

```
summary(linear)

##
## Call:
## lm(formula = y ~ x)
##
## Residuals:
##     Min      1Q  Median      3Q     Max
## -5.6481 -3.7122 -1.9390  0.9698 29.8283
##
## Coefficients:
##             Estimate Std. Error t value Pr(>|t|)
## (Intercept) -13.6323     1.6335  -8.345 4.63e-13 ***
```

```
## x             11.9801     0.7167  16.715   < 2e-16 ***
## ---
## Signif. codes:  0 '***' 0.001 '**' 0.01 '*' 0.05 '.' 0.1 ' ' 1
##
## Residual standard error: 6.51 on 98 degrees of freedom
## Multiple R-squared:  0.7403, Adjusted R-squared:  0.7377
## F-statistic: 279.4 on 1 and 98 DF,  p-value: < 2.2e-16
```

This code chunk is familiar territory. It takes some simulation data for x and y and then plots a best-fit linear model on top of it. This example uses 100% of the simulated data as its training set and looks at the model performance. For this particular view, a multiple R-squared of 0.74 isn't great. Let's try a version that splits the data by our standard 70/30 random sampling and see how it differs

First, let's split the data into a train-and-test set using simple random sampling:

```
data <- data.frame(x, y)

data.samples <- sample(1:nrow(data), nrow(data) * 0.7, replace = FALSE)

training.data <- data[data.samples, ]
test.data <- data[-data.samples, ]
```

Next, apply the linear model on the training data:

```
train.linear <- lm(y ~ x, training.data)
```

Now that you have a trained model, let's compare the model's output values to actual values. You can do this by using the `predict()` function in R, which takes the `train.linear` object and applies it to whatever data you supply it to it. Because your handy test data is available, you can use that to compare:

```
train.output <- predict(train.linear, test.data)
```

You've now used your test data, which has the same underlying behavior as the training data, to pass through your model and get some results. The test data has a dependent variable, x, and an independent variable, y. You need to use the dependent variable specifically for this evaluation because you want to compare what the model thinks the answer should be, given input x, compared to the actual values in your test set, given by y.

For regression specifically, you can do this in one of many ways, depending on the data and what kind of error analysis that you want to do specifically. In this case, you'll be using a test metric called the root-mean-square error, or RMSE:

$$\text{RMSE} = \sqrt{\left(\frac{1}{n}\Sigma\left(y_{predicted} - y_{actual}\right)^2\right)}$$

In plain English, the RMSE says that you take the output values that the model has provided for the training data input, subtract those by the y values that you have in the test data, square the values, divide those by the total number of observations *n*, sum up all the values, and, finally, take the square root. Here's what the code looks like:

```
RMSE.df = data.frame(predicted = train.output, actual = test.data$y,
    SE = ((train.output - test.data$y)^2/length(train.output)))

head(RMSE.df)

##      predicted    actual          SE
## 2    7.553671   6.383579 0.04563716
## 4   11.183322   7.233768 0.51996594
## 6   31.035159  39.640442 2.46836334
## 8   -4.938659   1.591971 1.42163749
## 9    2.041033   3.022771 0.03212698
## 11  25.108383  23.709676 0.06521277

sqrt(sum(RMSE.df$SE))

## [1] 5.90611
```

Consider the resultant RMSE value of 5.9 as this model's error score. To see just how good this number is, you must compare it to another RMSE value. You can run this same logic on a function fit of one higher degree and see what kind of RMSE you get out as the end result:

```
train.quadratic <- lm(y ~ x^2 + x, training.data)

quadratic.output <- predict(train.quadratic, test.data)

RMSE.quad.df = data.frame(predicted = quadratic.output, actual = test.data$y,
    SE = ((quadratic.output - test.data$y)^2/length(train.output)))

head(RMSE.quad.df)

##      predicted    actual          SE
## 2    7.553671   6.383579 0.04563716
## 4   11.183322   7.233768 0.51996594
## 6   31.035159  39.640442 2.46836334
## 8   -4.938659   1.591971 1.42163749
## 9    2.041033   3.022771 0.03212698
## 11  25.108383  23.709676 0.06521277

sqrt(sum(RMSE.quad.df$SE))

## [1] 5.90611
```

This output demonstrates that bumping up the polynomial degree fit by one to a quadratic helps to decrease the error in what the model is predicting (from the quad ratic.output variable) compared to what the actual values are. This follows intuitively from the fact that the actual data you're plotting appears to be fit well by a quadratic anyway.

The natural next step is to increase the polynomial degree even further and see how that affects the RMSE value:

```
train.polyn <- lm(y ~ poly(x, 4), training.data)

polyn.output <- predict(train.polyn, test.data)

RMSE.polyn.df = data.frame(predicted = polyn.output, actual = test.data$y,
    SE = ((polyn.output - test.data$y)^2/length(train.output)))

head(RMSE.polyn.df)

##       predicted    actual          SE
## 2     5.0313235  6.383579 0.060953156
## 4     7.0568495  7.233768 0.001043337
## 6    40.6367241 39.640442 0.033085916
## 8     0.7841328  1.591971 0.021753393
## 9     2.7506929  3.022771 0.002467546
## 11   24.2647775 23.709676 0.010271274

sqrt(sum(RMSE.polyn.df$SE))

## [1] 0.9357653
```

You can see that the RMSE has gone up compared to the quadratic fit case. This follows the same pattern of a higher-degree polynomial overfitting the data.

When we first learn about fitting a line to a series of data points in our early education, we don't tend to learn the intricacies of sampling techniques, nor splitting our data into training and test sets. When we first start out with regression fitting, we start with a straight line fit, as depicted in Figure 3-8.

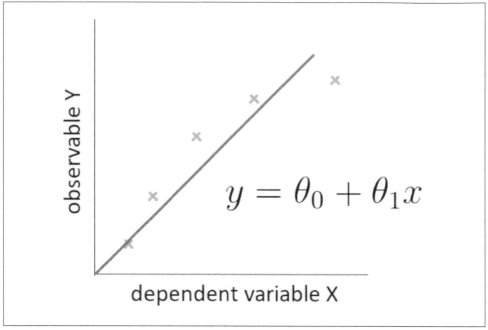

Figure 3-8. A simple linear fit to data will mostly be underfit; this is when the fitted line as given by the coefficients output from the model don't quite line up with the data you have

Figure 3-8 has some data, as denoted by the X marks, and the model fit, denoted by the line overlaid on top. There is also the equation that describes this model of $y = \theta_0 + \theta_1 x$, sometimes written as $y = b + mx$. There are two values that are given by the model fitting process, θ_0 and θ_1.

For this simple picture, we have a model that is pretty underfit to the data. Meaning: that the line on the chart that represents the machine learning model (simple linear regression) doesn't explain most of the data; it's too simple a model. Linear models can only ever underfit or well represent the data that you are plotting. If, for example, your cartoon model matched a series of data points that were a straight line, it would be an accurate representation. In a best-case scenario, linear regression can fit exactly to the data, but it is difficult for a simple procedure like this to overfit the data. Because linear models are difficult to overfit to the data, we rarely see the use of training and test sets to evaluate them. Sticking with the cartoon picture, if you were to add another data point that follows in roughly the same shape as what you see, the linear model will continue to diverge from it and not really produce an accurate picture in the long run.

Let's contrast the linear fit with a cartoon of a quadratic fit in Figure 3-9. The fit in this case is better than the linear case. The model fit tends to conform to the shape of most of the data points, and the model has become a little more complex. We have an equation that describes the model, and now you have more model-derived outputs to worry about. If you were to add another couple of data points to the picture in roughly the same shape, the quadratic looks like it will fit generally pretty well for the foreseeable future.

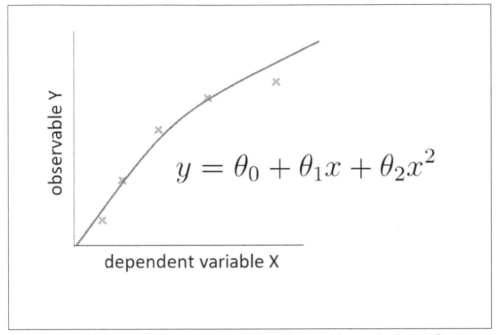

Figure 3-9. A quadratic fit has a slightly more complex model given by the coefficients that are output from the model; by training a machine learning model with a specific training sample and then looking at the difference between that and the saved test data, you can evaluate how well the model fit the data

Lastly, with some kind of complex model fit like the one seen in Figure 3-10, just about every data point is fit by the model exactly with no wiggle room. The downside of this is future explanatory power. If we follow the same logic as before and add a few more data points to the picture, the model shown won't fit them well at all and will have an increased error.

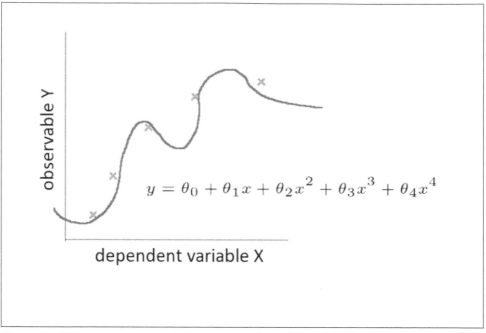

$$y = \theta_0 + \theta_1 x + \theta_2 x^2 + \theta_3 x^3 + \theta_4 x^4$$

Figure 3-10. In a complex model fit scenario, where the model is too specific to the training data, new test data that's applied to it will likely have high errors when we evaluate the model output versus our test data

When you do a train/test validation on continuous data as in the regression example here, you can choose from a host of statistical measures like the RMSE. Generally speaking, though, you want to compare the output values that the model gives you, based on a subset of data that you used to train the model, to that of the data you held out for testing purposes. You should have a list of numbers for the model estimates and a list of numbers that are the actual values. These will invariably have some kind of difference to them, which you can then bubble up to some aggregate number and compare against other methods.

For continuous data such as the type we've been testing with thus far, there are a few different statistical tests with which you can compare the error outputs of your results:

RMSE

$$\text{RMSE} = \sqrt{\frac{1}{n}\Sigma\left(y_{predicted} - y_{actual}\right)^2}$$

Mean Absolute Error (MAE)

$$\text{MAE} = \frac{1}{n} \Sigma \left| y_{predicted} - y_{actual} \right|$$

Root Relative Squared Error (RRSE)

$$\text{RRSE} = \sqrt{\frac{\Sigma \left(y_{predicted} - y_{actual} \right)^2}{\Sigma \left(\bar{y}_{predicted} - y_{actual} \right)^2}}$$

Relative Absolute Error (RAE)

$$\text{RAE} = \frac{\Sigma \left| y_{predicted} - y_{actual} \right|}{\Sigma \left| \bar{y}_{predicted} - y_{actual} \right|}$$

For RMSE and MAE, we look at the "average difference" between the model output, $y_{predicted}$ and the values we have in our test set, y_{actual}. These are compared at the same scale of our feature. You can think of it like 1 point of error is a difference of 1 between $y_{predicted}$ and y_{actual}.

In RRSE and RAE, we have a new variable of $\bar{y}_{predicted}$, which is the average value of our model output and is just a scalar number. These statistics divide the values of our predicted and actual data by the variation in our feature so that the end result is on a scale from 0 to 1. We tend to multiply this number by 100, so we get something in the 0 to 100 range and convert it into a percentage as a result. The denominators of the two equations tell us how much the feature deviates from its average value, which is why we call them "relative" errors.

Training and Test Sets: Classification Modeling

You evaluate a classification model's performance by starting with a "confusion matrix." In a simple form, it can take representation as a 2 × 2 matrix, in which the model output predicted classes are compared to the actual classes and the count of the model output in the cells of the matrix. This informs you as to how many true positives, true negatives, false positives, and false negatives there are as a result. As with regression statistics, classification statistics have many tools with which you can evaluate the final performance of the model. Let's take a look at some of them:

```
iris.df <- iris

iris.df$Species <- as.character(iris.df$Species)
```

```
iris.df$Species[iris.df$Species != "setosa"] <- "other"

iris.df$Species <- as.factor(iris.df$Species)

iris.samples <- sample(1:nrow(iris.df), nrow(iris.df) * 0.7,
    replace = FALSE)

training.iris <- iris.df[iris.samples, ]

test.iris <- iris.df[-iris.samples, ]

library(randomForest)

iris.rf <- randomForest(Species ~ ., data = training.iris)

iris.predictions <- predict(iris.rf, test.iris)

table(iris.predictions, test.iris$Species)

##
## iris.predictions other setosa
##          other     31     0
##          setosa     0    14
```

In a binary class truth table, there are two outcomes: either the predicted value is some class, or it isn't. In this case, you're focusing on whether the model predicted a setosa class or something else. There are four values for the confusion table:

True positives
> The model predicted setosa classes and got them right.

True negatives
> The model predicted other classes and got them right.

False positives
> The model predicted setosa classes, but the correct answer was other.

False negatives
> The model predicted other classes, but the correct answer was setosa.

The output from this truth table isn't super interesting, because it was so accurate. There were no incorrectly predicted classes. For the sake of illustration, though, let's assume that we had a confusion matrix output that was slightly inaccurate:

```
##
##           other setosa
##   other    28     3
##   setosa    2    12
```

This example forces two false positives and two false negatives. So now we have 15 true positives (TP), 26 true negatives (TN), 2 false positives (FP) and 3 false negatives

(FN). With classification models like these, we have a number of statistics from which we can choose to test our accuracy:

Sensitivity (equivalent to hit rate, or recall)

$$\text{Sensitivity} = \frac{TP}{TP + FN} = 0.83$$

Specificity

$$\text{Specificity} = \frac{TN}{TN + FP} = 0.92$$

Precision (or positive predictive value)

$$\text{Precision} = \frac{TP}{TP + FP} = 0.88$$

Accuracy

$$\text{Accuracy} = \frac{TP + TN}{TP + TN + FP + FN} = 0.89$$

F1 score

$$\text{F1} = \frac{2TP}{2TP + FP + FN} = 0.86$$

Many of these values are used as benchmarks for classification models. With regression models you had your handy RMSE value that you could compare against other models, so what would the corresponding go-to benchmark for accuracy be in this case? Let's walk through the available options:

Sensitivity
Often called *recall*, this is if you have a lower threshold set for your classification model. You would set a lower bar if you didn't want to miss out on any plants that could possibly be of a setosa type.

Specificity
Logically the same thing as precision, but for the opposite case when you're predicting whether a plant isn't a setosa variant.

Precision

The number of positive cases you've predicted divided by the total predicted positive. If you had a model that had a very high sensitivity, that would be akin to setting a threshold in your model to say, "Only classify a plant as `setosa` if we are absolutely sure about it."

Accuracy

Number of true cases divided by the total true and false cases.

F1 score

Weighted average of precision and recall scores.

You might be tempted to point out that your accuracy benchmark should just be the accuracy statistical measure outlined earlier. For the case in which you have an almost identical number of false positives and false negatives, this would be a perfectly fine measure to use. However, if the false positives or false negatives are skewed in favor of one or the other, you need a more robust statistical test to account for such behavior.

Although the F1 score might be less intuitive than accuracy at face value, it is generally more useful because F1 and accuracy are about the same number when the false positive and false negative rates are low. You can see the usefulness of the F1 score if you look at a few different mock models that have various precision and recall values. You might be tempted to just take the average of the precision and recall to get a performance metric, which you can see in Table 3-1.

Table 3-1. Tabular results of model outputs and related statistical measures of performance

Sensitivity (precision)	Recall	Average	F1 score
0.50	0.40	0.45	0.44
0.70	0.10	0.40	0.18
0.02	1.00	0.51	0.04
0.00	0.01	0.51	0.02
1.00	1.00	1.00	1.00

This example data demonstrates a few different models showing classification specificity and recall. If you wanted to evaluate the model's performance based on the average of these two numbers, that approach breaks down when you have either a high precision and low recall or opposite picture. However, the F1 score balances out those quirks and provides a more reliable metric with which to assess your classification model's performance.

Cross-Validation

So far, we've talked about how just running a model on 100% of your data could yield a result that doesn't generalize well to new incoming data. This was our motivation for splitting the data we start with into a training set, which usually takes about 70% of the data and a test set that comprises the rest. You unleash the model on the training data and then use the test set to check what the model's output is compared to the answers you have on hand.

This process of training and testing data is still somewhat limited, however. In one capacity, when you're testing the model output against the reserved data, you are seeing only what the error is for that exact grouping of the test data. In theory, the test data should be representative of the entire dataset as a whole, but in practice there are cases in which that might not be true. You should want to train the model in such a way that you can be sure the error is representative of the entire dataset, not just the specific slice you get from the randomly selected bits you put in the test set.

Cross-validation is a statistical technique by which you take your entire dataset, split it into a number of small train/test chunks, evaluate the error for each chunk, and then average those final errors. This approach winds up being a more accurate way of assessing whether your modeling approach has any issues that could be hidden in various combinations of the training and test parts of the dataset.

In fact we've already done one form of cross-validation! The simple 70/30 train/test split you did earlier in this chapter is called a simple "holdout" cross-validation technique. There are many other statistical cross-validation techniques, however, and with R having its basis in statistical design, you can model many different types of cross-validation.

k-Fold Cross-Validation

In contrast to holdout cross-validation, a much more commonly used technique is called *k*-fold cross-validation (see Figure 3-11). This involves taking your dataset and splitting it into k chunks. For each of these chunks, you then split the data into a smaller train/test set and then evaluate that individual chunk's error. After you have all the errors for all the chunks, you simply take the average. The advantage to this method is that you can then see the error in all aspects of your data instead of just testing on one specific subset of it.

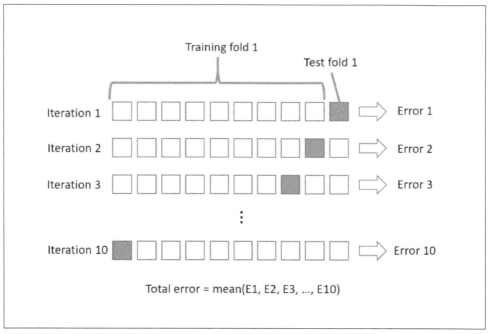

Figure 3-11. Cross-validation is the statistical practice of performing many training and test procedures on our data; this example shows a 10-fold cross-validation

In R, you can use the cut function to evenly split up a given dataset's indices for subsetting. You then simply loop over the applied folds of your data, doing the train/test split for each fold:

```
set.seed(123)

x <- rnorm(100, 2, 1)
y = exp(x) + rnorm(5, 0, 2)
data <- data.frame(x, y)

data.shuffled <- data[sample(nrow(data)), ]
folds <- cut(seq(1, nrow(data)), breaks = 10, labels = FALSE)

errors <- c(0)

for (i in 1:10) {
    fold.indexes <- which(folds == i, arr.ind = TRUE)

    test.data <- data[fold.indexes, ]
    training.data <- data[-fold.indexes, ]

    train.linear <- lm(y ~ x, training.data)
    train.output <- predict(train.linear, test.data)
    errors <- c(errors, sqrt(sum(((train.output - test.data$y)^2/
```

```
    length(train.output)))))
}

errors[2:11]

## [1]  4.696183  6.392002  4.769101  4.259850  9.634505  5.073442  7.547830
## [8]  7.366703  3.974609 10.539853

mean(errors[2:11])

## [1] 6.425408
```

Earlier in this chapter we looked at how a linear regression fit on example data gave us an error estimate around five or so. The preceding example shows that the error estimate can vary to a wide degree just within your own data depending on how you split the training and test sets! In this example, you can see the outputs for the RMSE values for 10 different cuts of the data. Some errors go as low as 3.9, others as high as 10.5. So by using cross-validation, not only can you see there is a high degree of variability in the RMSE of this data, but you can mitigate that by taking the average of those values to get a final number that's more representative of the error across the data as a whole.

Summary

In this chapter, we reviewed many statistical concepts that form the foundation for how we design our data to use in machine learning models. We first discussed various sampling techniques by which we take the dataset we start with and pick out values from it. You can do this randomly (which is the most common way) through the use of simple random sampling. There are other sampling techniques like stratified or cluster sampling that can arise but do so much more infrequently.

When you evaluate a machine learning model's performance, you need some baseline values to compare against what the model provides as its prediction. You do this by taking the starting data and splitting it into a training set and a test set. The training set is usually 70% of the total and the test set is the remaining 30%. You always want the training set to be much larger than the test set so that the model has enough data points to use for calculation purposes.

Evaluation of machine learning models comes in two forms: those for regression-based predictions, and those for classification-based predictions. For regression outputs, you typically get vectors of numbers against which you compare your test data. You can do this by using many statistical tests, one common form being the RMSE. With RMSE, you take the model output values, subtract the test values, square the differences, take the mean, and then calculate the square root of the final result. This tends to give us a flexible but accurate picture of the model output.

Finally, we discussed techniques related to cross-validation. This is a statistical technique wherein you effectively split the data into many small training and test sets, evaluate them independently, and then aggregate their errors. This allows you to be more confident in the model's error outputs in that you know it has been applied to the entire dataset instead of a small view of it. This practice is a good way to ensure statistical validity of your machine learning model.

## CHAPTER 4

Regression in a Nutshell

In Chapter 1, in which we briefly explored the realms of machine learning, we began with linear regression because it is probably something that you have come across at some point in your mathematical training. The process is fairly intuitive and easier to explain as a first concept than some other machine learning models. Additionally, many realms of data analysis rely on regression modeling ranging from a business trying to forecast its profits, to the frontiers of science trying to figure out new discoveries governing the laws of the universe. We can find regression in any scenario in which a prediction against time is needed. In this chapter, we examine how to use regression modeling in R to a deep extent, but we also explore some caveats and pitfalls to be aware of in the process.

The main motivation behind regression is to build an equation by which we can learn more about our data. There is no hard-and-fast rule about which type of regression model to fit to your data, however. Choosing between a logistic regression, linear regression, or multivariate regression model depends on the problem and the data that you have. You could fit a straight line to a given series of data points, but is that always the best case? Ideally, we are after a balance of simplicity and explanatory power. A straight line fit to a complex series of data might be simple, but might not describe the whole picture. On the other hand, having a very simple set of data that is basically a straight line and fitting a model with all sorts of wacky curves to it might give you a very high degree of accuracy, but leave very little room for new data points to be fit to it.

You might recall in your high school mathematics education about having a couple points of data and fitting a line through it. This fit to data is the easiest form of machine learning and is used often without realizing it is a type of machine learning. Although fitting a line to two data points is relatively easy to learn, fitting a line with three or more data points becomes a task better suited for computers to handle from a computation perspective. Simply adding one more data point (or, as we'll see, several dozen more) makes the problem much more difficult to solve. But through mathematical techniques that power mainstream machine learning models, we can compute those kinds of problems very easily. R makes a lot of these steps quite simple to compute, and this chapter provides a foundation for assessing questions about where we draw the line between model complexity and accuracy.

Linear Regression

In Chapter 1, we briefly encountered linear regression with an example of the mtcars dataset. In that example, we determined a linear relationship of fuel efficiency as a function of vehicle weight and saw the trend go downward. We extracted coefficients for a linear mathematical equation and dusted our hands. Yet, there is a lot more beyond simply slapping an equation onto a bunch of data and calling it a day. Let's revisit our mtcars example (Figure 4-1):

```
model <- lm(mtcars$mpg ~ mtcars$disp)

plot(y = mtcars$mpg, x = mtcars$disp, xlab = "Engine Size (cubic inches)",
     ylab = "Fuel Efficiency (Miles per Gallon)", main = "Fuel Efficiency From
the `mtcars` Dataset")

abline(a = coef(model[1]), b = coef(model)[2], lty = 2)
```

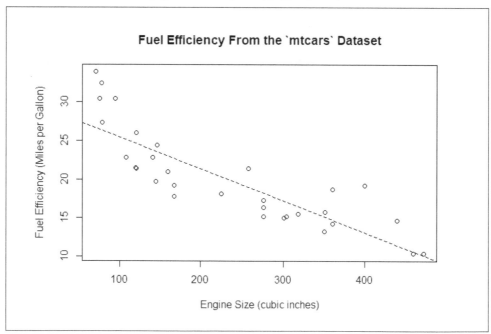

Figure 4-1. A simple linear regression fit to data

Let's revisit our `mtcars` example (Figure 4-1), where we model the fuel efficiency (`mpg`) as a function of engine size (`disp`) and then look at the outputs of the model with the `summary` function:

```
summary(model)

##
## Call:
## lm(formula = mtcars$mpg ~ mtcars$disp)
##
## Residuals:
##     Min      1Q  Median      3Q     Max
## -4.8922 -2.2022 -0.9631  1.6272  7.2305
##
## Coefficients:
##                  Estimate Std. Error t value Pr(>|t|)
## (Intercept) 29.599855   1.229720  24.070  < 2e-16 ***
## mtcars$disp -0.041215   0.004712  -8.747 9.38e-10 ***
## ---
## Signif. codes:  0 '***' 0.001 '**' 0.01 '*' 0.05 '.' 0.1 ' ' 1
##
## Residual standard error: 3.251 on 30 degrees of freedom
## Multiple R-squared:  0.7183, Adjusted R-squared:  0.709
## F-statistic: 76.51 on 1 and 30 DF,  p-value: 9.38e-10
```

There is a wealth of information dumped out from the `summary()` function call on this linear model object. Generally, the one number people will typically look at to get a baseline accuracy assessment is the multiple R-squared value. The closer that value is to 1, the more accurate the linear regression model is. There are a lot of other terms in this output, though, so let's walk through each element to gain a solid understanding:

Call
> This displays the formulaic function call we used. In this case, we used one response variable, `mpg`, as a function of one dependent variable, `disp`, both of which were being called from the `mtcars` data frame.

Residuals
> Residuals are a measure of vertical distance from each data point to the fitted line in our model. In this case, we have summary statistics for all of the vertical distances for all of our points relative to the fitted line. The smaller this value is, the better the fit is.

Coefficients
> These are the estimates for the coefficients of our linear equation. Our equation in this case would be $y = 0.04x + 29.59$.

- Std. Error: With those coefficients come error estimates as given by the Std. Error part of the coefficients table. In reality, our equation would be something like $y = (-0.04 \pm 0.005)x + (29.59 \pm 1.23)$.

- t-value: This is the measurement of the difference relative to the variation in our data. This value is linked with p-values, but p-values are used far more frequently.

- p-value: p-values are statistical assessments of significance. The workings of p-values are more complicated than that, but for our purposes a p-value being of value less than 0.05 means that we can take the number as being statistically significant. If the number in question has a p-value greater than 0.05, we should err on the side of it not being statistically significant. The star ratings next to them are explained by the significance codes that follow.

Residual standard error

This error estimate pertains to the standard deviation of our data.

Multiple R-squared

This is the R-squared value for when we have multiple predictors. This isn't totally relevant for our linear example, but when we add more predictors to the model, invariably our multiple R-squared will go up. This is because some feature we add to the model will explain some part of the variance, whether its true or not.

Adjusted R-squared

To counteract the biases introduced from having a constantly increasing R-squared value with more predictors, the adjusted R-squared tends to be a better representation of a model's accuracy when there's multiple features.

F-statistic

Finally, the F-statistic is the ratio of the variance explained by parameters in the model and the unexplained variance.

This simple linear example has some decent explanatory power. We have determined a relationship between fuel efficiency and engine size. Oftentimes, this is where simple linear regression examples exhaust their usefulness. The things we are most after in this specific case are the slope and intercept. If this example were applied to sales over time, for example, our output from this modeling exercise would be a starting value for the intercept, and a growth rate for the coefficient.

Multivariate Regression

Suppose that you want to build a more robust model of fuel efficiency with more variables built into it. Fuel efficiency of a vehicle can be a complex phenomenon with many contributing factors other than engine size, so finding all of the features that are responsible for driving the behavior of the model in the most accurate fashion is where you want to utilize regression as you have been, but in a multivariate context.

Recall that our simple linear regression example was based around:

$$y = b + m_1 x_1$$

where the coefficients are the intercept, b, and the slope, m, tied to the one variable we had in the model. If you want to bring in more factors that contribute to the model, change the mathematical form to:

$$y = b + m_1 x_1 + m_2 x_2 + m_3 x_3 + (...)$$

where x_1, x_2, x_3, and so forth, are different features in the model, such as a vehicle's weight, engine size, number of cylinders, and so on. Because the new objective is to find coefficients for a model of the form $y = f(x_1, x_2, x_3, (...))$, you need to revisit the call to the lm() function in R:

```
lm.wt <- lm(mpg ~ disp + wt, data = mtcars)
summary(lm.wt)

##
## Call:
## lm(formula = mpg ~ disp + wt, data = mtcars)
##
## Residuals:
##     Min      1Q  Median      3Q     Max
## -3.4087 -2.3243 -0.7683  1.7721  6.3484
##
## Coefficients:
##             Estimate Std. Error t value Pr(>|t|)
## (Intercept) 34.96055    2.16454  16.151 4.91e-16 ***
## disp        -0.01773    0.00919  -1.929  0.06362 .
## wt          -3.35082    1.16413  -2.878  0.00743 **
## ---
## Signif. codes:  0 '***' 0.001 '**' 0.01 '*' 0.05 '.' 0.1 ' ' 1
##
## Residual standard error: 2.917 on 29 degrees of freedom
## Multiple R-squared:  0.7809, Adjusted R-squared:  0.7658
## F-statistic: 51.69 on 2 and 29 DF,  p-value: 2.744e-10
```

This code extends the linear modeling from earlier to include the vehicle's weight in the model fitting procedure. In this case, what you see is that the adjusted R-squared has gone up slightly from 0.709 when you fit a model of just the engine size, to 0.7658 after including the engine weight in the fit. However, notice that the statistical relevance of the previous feature has gone down considerably. Before, the p-value of the wt feature was far below the 0.05 threshold for a p-value to be significant; now it's 0.06. This might be due to the vehicle fuel efficiency being more sensitive to changes in vehicle weight than engine size.

If you want to extend this analysis further, you can bring in another feature from the dataset and see how the R-squared of the model and *p*-values of the coefficients change accordingly:

```
lm.cyl <- lm(mpg ~ disp + wt + cyl, data = mtcars)
summary(lm.cyl)
```

```
##
## Call:
## lm(formula = mpg ~ disp + wt + cyl, data = mtcars)
##
## Residuals:
##     Min      1Q  Median      3Q     Max
## -4.4035 -1.4028 -0.4955  1.3387  6.0722
##
## Coefficients:
##               Estimate Std. Error t value Pr(>|t|)
## (Intercept) 41.107678   2.842426  14.462 1.62e-14 ***
## disp         0.007473   0.011845   0.631  0.53322
## wt          -3.635677   1.040138  -3.495  0.00160 **
## cyl         -1.784944   0.607110  -2.940  0.00651 **
## ---
## Signif. codes:  0 '***' 0.001 '**' 0.01 '*' 0.05 '.' 0.1 ' ' 1
##
## Residual standard error: 2.595 on 28 degrees of freedom
## Multiple R-squared:  0.8326, Adjusted R-squared:  0.8147
## F-statistic: 46.42 on 3 and 28 DF,  p-value: 5.399e-11
```

This code takes the same approach as before, but adds the engine's cylinder count to the model. Notice that the R-squared value has increased yet again from 0.709 to 0.8147. However, the statistical relevancy of the displacement in the data is basically defunct, with a *p*-value 10 times the threshold at 0.53322 instead of closer to 0.05. This tells us that the fuel efficiency is tied more to the combined feature set of vehicle weight and number of cylinders than it is to the engine size. You can rerun this analysis with just the statistically relevant features:

```
lm.cyl.wt <- lm(mpg ~ wt + cyl, data = mtcars)
summary(lm.cyl.wt)
```

```
##
## Call:
## lm(formula = mpg ~ wt + cyl, data = mtcars)
##
## Residuals:
##     Min      1Q  Median      3Q     Max
## -4.2893 -1.5512 -0.4684  1.5743  6.1004
##
## Coefficients:
##               Estimate Std. Error t value Pr(>|t|)
## (Intercept)  39.6863     1.7150  23.141  < 2e-16 ***
## wt           -3.1910     0.7569  -4.216 0.000222 ***
```

```
## cyl            -1.5078      0.4147  -3.636 0.001064 **
## ---
## Signif. codes:  0 '***' 0.001 '**' 0.01 '*' 0.05 '.' 0.1 ' ' 1
##
## Residual standard error: 2.568 on 29 degrees of freedom
## Multiple R-squared:  0.8302, Adjusted R-squared:  0.8185
## F-statistic: 70.91 on 2 and 29 DF,  p-value: 6.809e-12
```

By removing the statistically irrelevant feature from the model, you have more or less preserved the R-squared accuracy at 0.8185 versus 0.8147, while maintaining only relevant features to the data.

You should take care when adding features to the data, however. In R, you can easily model a response to all the features in the data by calling the lm() function with the following form:

```
lm.all <- lm(mpg ~ ., data = mtcars)
summary(lm.all)

##
## Call:
## lm(formula = mpg ~ ., data = mtcars)
##
## Residuals:
##     Min     1Q Median     3Q     Max
## -3.4506 -1.6044 -0.1196  1.2193  4.6271
##
## Coefficients:
##             Estimate Std. Error t value Pr(>|t|)
## (Intercept) 12.30337   18.71788   0.657   0.5181
## cyl         -0.11144    1.04502  -0.107   0.9161
## disp         0.01334    0.01786   0.747   0.4635
## hp          -0.02148    0.02177  -0.987   0.3350
## drat         0.78711    1.63537   0.481   0.6353
## wt          -3.71530    1.89441  -1.961   0.0633 .
## qsec         0.82104    0.73084   1.123   0.2739
## vs           0.31776    2.10451   0.151   0.8814
## am           2.52023    2.05665   1.225   0.2340
## gear         0.65541    1.49326   0.439   0.6652
## carb        -0.19942    0.82875  -0.241   0.8122
## ---
## Signif. codes:  0 '***' 0.001 '**' 0.01 '*' 0.05 '.' 0.1 ' ' 1
##
## Residual standard error: 2.65 on 21 degrees of freedom
## Multiple R-squared:  0.869,  Adjusted R-squared:  0.8066
## F-statistic: 13.93 on 10 and 21 DF,  p-value: 3.793e-07
```

This syntax creates a linear model with the dependent variable mpg being modeled against everything in the dataset, as denoted by the . mark in the function call. The problem with this approach, however, is that you see very little statistical value in the coefficients of the model. Likewise, the standard error for each of the coefficients is very high, and thus pinning down an exact value for the coefficients is very difficult. Instead of this top-down approach to seeing which features are the most important in the dataset, it is better to approach it from the bottom up as we have done thus far. Although the theme of feature selection itself is a very broad topic—one which we explore in depth with other machine learning algorithms—we can mitigate some of these problems in a couple of ways:

Careful selection of features
> Pick features to add to the model one at a time and cut the ones that are statistically insignificant. We've accomplished this in the preceding code chunks by adding one parameter at a time and checking to see whether the *p*-value of the model output for that parameter is statistically significant.

Regularization
> Keep all of the features but mathematically reduce the coefficients of the less important ones to minimize their impact on the model.

Regularization

Regularization can be a tough concept mathematically, but in principle it's fairly straightforward. The idea is that you want to include as many of the features in your data as you can squeeze into the final model. The more features, the better you can explain all the intricacies of the dataset. The catch here is that the degree to which each feature explains part of the model, after regularization is applied, can be quite different.

Through the use of regularization, you can make your model more succinct and reduce the noise in the dataset that might be coming from features that have little impact on what you are trying to model against.

Let's see what the linear model for the `mtcars` dataset would look like if we included all the features. We would have an equation like this:

$$mpg = 12.3 - 0.11cyl + 0.01disp - 0.02hp + 0.79drat - 3.72wt + 0.82qsec + 0.31vs + 2.42am + 0.66gear - 0.20carb$$

According to this linear equation, fuel efficiency is most sensitive to the weight of the vehicle (-3.72*wt*), given that this one has the largest coefficient. However, most of these are all within an order of magnitude or so to one another. Regularization would keep all of the features, but the less important ones would have their coefficients scaled down much further.

To utilize this regularization technique, you call a particular type of regression modeling, known as a *lasso* regression, as shown here:

```
library(lasso2)
lm.lasso <- l1ce(mpg ~ ., data = mtcars)
summary(lm.lasso)$coefficients
```

```
##                  Value  Std. Error     Z score    Pr(>|Z|)
## (Intercept) 36.01809203 18.92587647  1.90311355 0.05702573
## cyl         -0.86225790  1.12177221 -0.76865686 0.44209704
## disp         0.00000000  0.01912781  0.00000000 1.00000000
## hp          -0.01399880  0.02384398 -0.58709992 0.55713660
## drat         0.05501092  1.78394922  0.03083659 0.97539986
## wt          -2.68868427  2.05683876 -1.30719254 0.19114733
## qsec         0.00000000  0.75361628  0.00000000 1.00000000
## vs           0.00000000  2.31605743  0.00000000 1.00000000
## am           0.44530641  2.14959278  0.20715850 0.83588608
## gear         0.00000000  1.62955841  0.00000000 1.00000000
## carb        -0.09506985  0.91237207 -0.10420075 0.91701004
```

This code calls the l1ce() function from the lasso2 package on the mtcars dataset. This uses the same function call that we want the fuel efficiency variable mpg modeled as a function of all the other variables in the dataset. Built in to lasso regression is the regularization technique, which is only applied during the heavy mathematical lifting part of the algorithm. The regularization part of the regression scales the coefficients according to how much actual impact they have on the model in a more statistical fashion. In some cases, this can result in some features being scaled down to such a low value that they are approximated as zero. As a result of this regression modeling, you now have a different equation:

mpg = 36.02 − 0.86cyl + 0disp − 0.014hp + 0.06drat − 2.69wt + 0qsec + 0vs + 0.45am + 0gear − 0.095carb

Or, more simply:

mpg = 36.02 − 0.86cyl − 0.014hp + 0.06drat − 2.69wt + 0.45am + − 0.095carb

The most important feature before the change to a lasso regression was the vehicle's weight, wt, which has remained unchanged as far as its relative importance. Even though the coefficient has changed somewhat, the fact that it is the highest magnitude coefficient remains the same. What you see in terms of less useful features being scaled down—in this case to zero—are features that you would probably think have little impact on fuel efficiency to begin with. Quarter-mile drag race time (qsec), engine configuration in terms of a V-shape or a straight-line shape (vs), and number of forward gears (gear) have all been rescaled down to zero.

However, the variable of displacement showed a clear relationship to fuel efficiency that we saw earlier. It being scaled down to zero does not mean there is *no* relationship whatsoever between just that one variable and our response, but when taken together with all the other variables in the dataset, its importance is negligible.

Remember, in this case we are interested in a model of *all* features, not necessarily the importance of just *one* feature.

Notice from the new lasso regression model that some of the coefficients have been more or less mathematically eliminated from the model. To further refine the model and reduce the number of features in it, you can rerun the regression without those features and see what changes:

```
lm.lasso2 <- l1ce(mpg ~ cyl + hp + wt + am + carb, data = mtcars)
summary(lm.lasso2)$coefficients
```

```
##                    Value Std. Error    Z score      Pr(>|Z|)
## (Intercept) 31.2819166926 4.51160542  6.93365527 4.100942e-12
## cyl         -0.7864202230 0.86107128 -0.91330444 3.610824e-01
## hp          -0.0009037003 0.02343634 -0.03855979 9.692414e-01
## wt          -1.9248597501 1.38749433 -1.38729198 1.653527e-01
## am           0.0000000000 2.22143917  0.00000000 1.000000e+00
## carb         0.0000000000 0.67947216  0.00000000 1.000000e+00
```

With the reduced dataset being then passed into another lasso regression, you can see that the transmission type of the car, am, and the number of carburetors, carb, have both dropped to zero. By removing these features and rerunning, you can see if any more drop out:

```
lm.lasso3 <- l1ce(mpg ~ cyl + hp + wt, data = mtcars)
summary(lm.lasso3)$coefficients
```

```
##                 Value Std. Error     Z score Pr(>|Z|)
## (Intercept) 30.2106931 1.97117597 15.3262284 0.0000000
## cyl         -0.7220771 0.82941877 -0.8705821 0.3839824
## hp           0.0000000 0.01748364  0.0000000 1.0000000
## wt          -1.7568469 1.07478525 -1.6346028 0.1021324
```

In this case, the horsepower of the car, hp, has now dropped out. You can continue to run as long as you have multiple features to test against:

```
lm.lasso4 <- l1ce(mpg ~ cyl + wt, data = mtcars)
summary(lm.lasso4)$coefficients
```

```
##                 Value Std. Error    Z score Pr(>|Z|)
## (Intercept) 29.8694933  1.4029760 21.290096 0.0000000
## cyl         -0.6937847  0.5873288 -1.181254 0.2375017
## wt          -1.7052064  1.0720172 -1.590652 0.1116879
```

The final result is a model that has only two features instead of the 11 you started with:

$$mpg = 29.87 \quad 0.69cyl \quad 1.70wt$$

Polynomial Regression

Polynomial regression is simply fitting a higher degree function to the data. Previously, we've seen fits to our data along the following form:

$$y = b + m_1 x_1 + m_2 x_2 + m_3 x_3 (...)$$

Polynomial regression differs from the simple linear cases by having multiple degrees for each feature in the dataset. The form of which could be represented as follows:

$$y = b + m x_2$$

The following example will help with our reasoning (Figure 4-2):

```
pop <- data.frame(uspop)
pop$uspop <- as.numeric(pop$uspop)
pop$year <- seq(from = 1790, to = 1970, by = 10)

plot(y = pop$uspop, x = pop$year, main = "United States Population From 1790 to
1970",
    xlab = "Year", ylab = "Population")
```

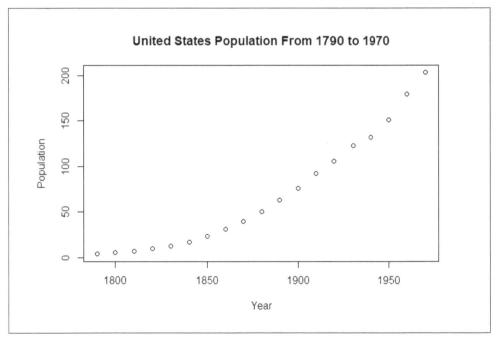

Figure 4-2. The plotted population of the United States in decades from 1790 to 1970

Here, we have a built-in dataset in R that we've tweaked slightly for demonstration purposes. Normally the uspop is a time–series object that has its own plotting criteria, but here we've tuned it to plot just the data points. This data is the population of the United States in 10-year periods from 1790 to 1970. Let's begin by fitting a linear model to the data:

```
lm1 <- lm(pop$uspop ~ pop$year)
summary(lm1)


##
## Call:
## lm(formula = pop$uspop ~ pop$year)
##
## Residuals:
##     Min      1Q  Median      3Q     Max
## -19.569 -14.776  -2.933   9.501  36.345
##
## Coefficients:
##                 Estimate Std. Error t value Pr(>|t|)
## (Intercept) -1.958e+03  1.428e+02  -13.71 1.27e-10 ***
## pop$year     1.079e+00  7.592e-02   14.21 7.29e-11 ***
## ---
## Signif. codes:  0 '***' 0.001 '**' 0.01 '*' 0.05 '.' 0.1 ' ' 1
##
## Residual standard error: 18.12 on 17 degrees of freedom
## Multiple R-squared:  0.9223, Adjusted R-squared:  0.9178
## F-statistic: 201.9 on 1 and 17 DF,  p-value: 7.286e-11
```

This simple linear fit of the data seems to work pretty well. The p-values of the estimates are very low, indicating a good statistical significance. Likewise, the R-squared values are both very good. However, the residuals show a pretty wide degree of variability, ranging as much as a difference of 36, as demonstrated in Figure 4-3:

```
plot(y = pop$uspop, x = pop$year, main = "United States Population From 1790 to
1970",
    xlab = "Year", ylab = "Population")

abline(a = coef(lm1[1]), b = coef(lm1)[2], lty = 2, col = "red")
```

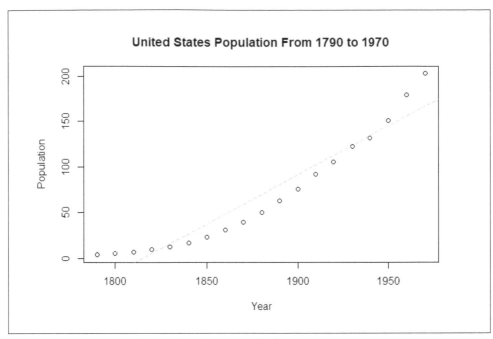

Figure 4-3. Population data with a linear model fit

The dotted line fit from the linear model seems to do OK. It fits some of the data better than others, but it's pretty clear from the data that it's not exactly a linear relationship. Moreover, we know from intuition that population over time tends to be more of an exponential shape than one that's a straight line. What you want to do next is to see how a model of a higher degree stacks up against the linear case, which is the lowest-order degree polynomial that you can fit:

```
lm2 <- lm(pop$uspop ~ poly(pop$year, 2))
summary(lm2)

##
## Call:
## lm(formula = pop$uspop ~ poly(pop$year, 2))
##
## Residuals:
##     Min      1Q  Median      3Q     Max
## -6.5997 -0.7105  0.2669  1.4065  3.9879
##
## Coefficients:
##                    Estimate Std. Error t value Pr(>|t|)
## (Intercept)         69.7695     0.6377  109.40  < 2e-16 ***
## poly(pop$year, 2)1 257.5420     2.7798   92.65  < 2e-16 ***
## poly(pop$year, 2)2  73.8974     2.7798   26.58 1.14e-14 ***
## ---
## Signif. codes:  0 '***' 0.001 '**' 0.01 '*' 0.05 '.' 0.1 ' ' 1
```

```
##
## Residual standard error: 2.78 on 16 degrees of freedom
## Multiple R-squared:  0.9983, Adjusted R-squared:  0.9981
## F-statistic:  4645 on 2 and 16 DF,  p-value: < 2.2e-16
```

This code calls the lm() function again, but this time with an extra parameter around the dependent variable, the poly() function. This function takes the date data and computes an orthogonal vector, which is then scaled appropriately. By default, the poly() function doesn't change the values of the date data, but you can use it to see if it yields any better results than the lower-order fit that you did previously. Recall that the linear fit is technically a polynomial, but of degree 1. In an equation, here's the resultant model fit:

$$y = b + m_1 x_1^2 + m_2 x_1$$

Let's slowly walk through the summary() output first. Looking at the residual output gives us a bit of relief: no residuals in the range of 30! Smaller residuals are always better in terms of model fit. The coefficients table now has three entries: one for the intercept, one of the first-degree term, and now one for the second-degree term. When you called poly(pop$year, 2), you instructed R that you want a polynomial of the date data with the highest degree being 2. Going back to the coefficients table, you can see that all of the p-values are statistically significant, which is also a good indication that this is a solid model fit to your data (see Figure 4-4):

```
plot(y = pop$uspop, x = pop$year, main = "United States Population From 1790 to 1970",
     xlab = "Year", ylab = "Population")

pop$lm2.predict = predict(lm2, newdata = pop)

lines(sort(pop$year), fitted(lm2)[order(pop$year)], col = "blue",
      lty = 2)
```

From Figure 4-4, it looks pretty obvious that the higher degree polynomial (in this case a quadratic equation) fits the data better. Clearly using higher degree polynomials works better than lower degree ones, right? What happens if you fit a third-degree polynomial? Or something higher still? I'll bet that if you use a sixth-degree polynomial you would have a very accurate model indeed! What immediately leaps out is that the simple linear fit that you had earlier fit the data as best it could, but the higher second-degree polynomial (i.e., a simple quadratic) fit better. A better way to distinguish the difference between higher-order polynomial fits is by looking at plots of each model's residuals, which you can see in Figure 4-5.

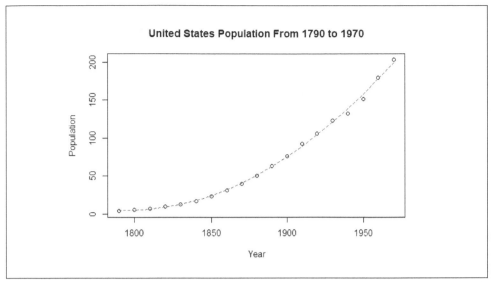

Figure 4-4. Population over time modeled with a quadratic fit seems to fit the data much better than a linear one; if you want the most accurate model possible, however, you might want to increase the polynomial degree to which you fit the data

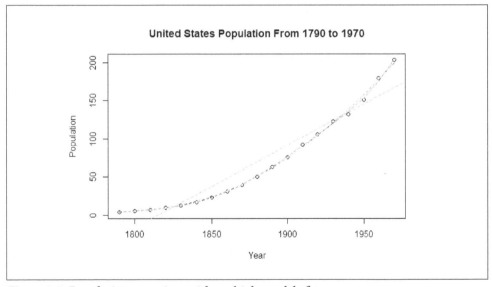

Figure 4-5. Population over time with multiple models fit

Figure 4-5 shows the linear fit compared to increasing degree polynomials. The polynomials are difficult to separate in terms of how well they fit, but all seem to fit better than the linear case. To compare models that are close approximations visually at this level, you would need to dive into looking at plots of their residuals instead, as demonstrated in Figure 4-6:

```
par(mfrow = c(2, 3))
plot(resid(lm1), main = "Degree 1", xlab = "Sequential Year",
    ylab = "Fit Residual")
plot(resid(lm2), main = "Degree 2", xlab = "Sequential Year",
    ylab = "Fit Residual")
plot(resid(lm3), main = "Degree 3", xlab = "Sequential Year",
    ylab = "Fit Residual")
plot(resid(lm4), main = "Degree 4", xlab = "Sequential Year",
    ylab = "Fit Residual")
plot(resid(lm5), main = "Degree 5", xlab = "Sequential Year",
    ylab = "Fit Residual")
plot(resid(lm6), main = "Degree 6", xlab = "Sequential Year",
    ylab = "Fit Residual")
```

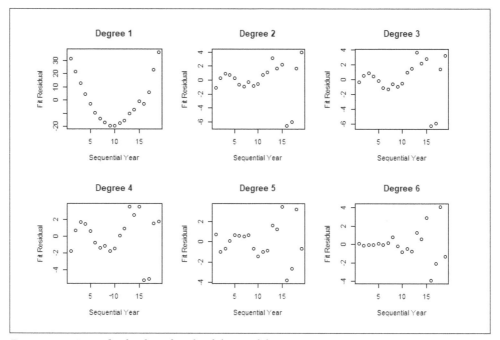

Figure 4-6. A residuals plot of each of the models

Recall that a residual is the vertical distance between a data point and the fitted model line. A model that fits the data points exactly should have a residuals plot as close to a flat line as possible. In the case of your linear fit, the scale of the residuals plot is much larger than the rest, and you can see that the linear fit has some pretty bad residual distance at its start, halfway point, and end. This is not an ideal model. On the other hand, the higher-degree polynomials seem to do pretty well. The scale of their residual plots are much nicer, but the one that really stands out is the sixth-degree polynomial fit at the end. The residuals plot is pretty much zero to start, and then it becomes a little more error-prone.

This is all well and good, but it might be easier to rank the model fit by looking at their residuals numerically:

```
c(sum(abs(resid(lm1))), sum(abs(resid(lm2))), sum(abs(resid(lm3))),
    sum(abs(resid(lm4))), sum(abs(resid(lm5))), sum(abs(resid(lm6))))

## [1] 272.51432  33.77224  34.54039  36.95125  25.45242  19.59938
```

This code sums the residual plots by absolute value of the residual. If you just take the raw sum of the residuals, you get an inaccurate picture because some residuals might be negative. So the total residual for the linear fit is quantitatively bad compared to the rest of the models, with the sixth-degree polynomial being the clear winner in terms of the best fit to the data points.

But is the best fit to the data points actually the best model? We must take into account the ideas of overfitting and underfitting the data. The linear model fit to the data in the previous case would be a good example of an underfit scenario. Clearly there's some structure in the data that isn't being explained by a simple linear fit. On the other hand, a model can be overfit if it is too specific to the data presented and offers little explanatory power for any new data that might come into the system. This is the risk you run by increasing the degree of polynomial models.

Goodness of Fit with Data—The Perils of Overfitting

We have just run an example of trying to get a model that has the best fit to our data. This is a good goal to have, but you need to be careful not to go *too* far in fitting perfectly to the data. We have seen so far that the linear fit to a population curve probably isn't the best model for the job. A quadratic or a cubic polynomial fit seems to do much better by comparison. Yet, is it worth it to keep increasing the degree of the model fit? Is the minimization of the residual the only goal in terms of selecting the best model for the job?

Root-Mean-Square Error

In statistics, the root-mean-square error (RMSE) is a quantifiable way to see how our model's predicted values stack up against actual values. Mathematically, the RMSE is given as follows:

$$\text{RMSE} = \sqrt{\left\langle \left(\text{predicted value} - \text{actual value}\right)^2 \right\rangle}$$

To assess polynomial fits, you can perform an RMSE analysis on each one. You can then compare the resultant errors and select the one that has the lowest result. To do so, you need new data that isn't in your model. For that, let's use the US population census data from 1980 to 2010:

```
uspop.2020 <- data.frame(year = c(1980, 1990, 2000, 2010), uspop = c(226.5,
    249.6, 282.2, 309.3))
uspop.2020.predict <- uspop.2020

pop2 <- data.frame(uspop)
pop2$uspop <- as.numeric(pop$uspop)
pop2$year <- seq(from = 1790, to = 1970, by = 10)
```

This code also reinitializes the old population data for prediction purposes as a general cleanup measure. From there, you can do your usual prediction routine, and then calculate the RMSE for each polynomial:

```
uspop.2020.predict$lm1 <- predict(lm(uspop ~ poly(year, 1), data = pop2),
    uspop.2020)

uspop.2020.predict$lm2 <- predict(lm(uspop ~ poly(year, 2), data = pop2),
    uspop.2020)

uspop.2020.predict$lm3 <- predict(lm(uspop ~ poly(year, 3), data = pop2),
    uspop.2020)

uspop.2020.predict$lm4 <- predict(lm(uspop ~ poly(year, 4), data = pop2),
    uspop.2020)

uspop.2020.predict$lm5 <- predict(lm(uspop ~ poly(year, 5), data = pop2),
    uspop.2020)

uspop.2020.predict$lm6 <- predict(lm(uspop ~ poly(year, 6), data = pop2),
    uspop.2020)
```

And, finally, calculate the RMSE:

```
c(sqrt(mean((uspop.2020.predict$uspop - uspop.2020.predict$lm1)^2)),
    sqrt(mean((uspop.2020.predict$uspop - uspop.2020.predict$lm2)^2)),
    sqrt(mean((uspop.2020.predict$uspop - uspop.2020.predict$lm3)^2)),
    sqrt(mean((uspop.2020.predict$uspop - uspop.2020.predict$lm4)^2)),
    sqrt(mean((uspop.2020.predict$uspop - uspop.2020.predict$lm5)^2)),
    sqrt(mean((uspop.2020.predict$uspop - uspop.2020.predict$lm6)^2)))

## [1]  75.622445   8.192311   5.070814   9.153189  73.632318 124.429798
```

From these results, you can see that the simple linear fit had an RMSE of 75, the second-degree polynomial had 8, and the third-degree polynomial had 5. The errors blow up after the third-degree polynomial, which is another indication that the models were too overfit to the data. In this case, you would select the model that has the lowest RMSE to the new predicted data by picking the polynomial of degree three.

Model Simplicity and Goodness of Fit

If you recall the model coefficients, each one has an attached *p*-value of statistical significance tied to it from the `lm()` model fitting procedure. If a coefficient's *p*-value is less than 0.05, it's safe to assume that it is statistically important for your model.

To help you to decide which model to use, identify where the trade-off is between model accuracy and model complexity. The more complex your model is—that is, the degree of polynomial used—the tighter it's going to fit to your data, but you run the risk of some of the coefficients being less statistically valid as the model becomes more complex. To avoid this, first look at both the R-squared and the number of statistically valid coefficients for each of your models:

```
table((summary(lm1)$coefficients[, 4]) < 0.05)

##
## TRUE
##    2

summary(lm1)$r.squared

## [1] 0.9223434
```

This example takes the coefficients from the simple linear fit, `lm1`, and then extracts the *p*-values tied to the coefficients. It then tabularizes how many of those are statistically valid (if they are above 0.05). The result from the simple linear case is that there are two coefficients: the slope and the intercept, and that they are both statistically valid. The R-squared value also confirms that the fit is pretty good, but let's use that as a baseline for the sake of comparison.

Instead of computing this for each model and looking back and forth at the results, you can dump all this information into a handy data frame for easier readability. Let's define a `model.order` as the highest degree of the polynomial fit (this is simply the number you pass into the `poly()` function during the linear model `lm()` function call). You then define `coef.true` as the number of coefficients that are statistically valid in the model. In this case, you are looking only at the coefficients related to the dependent variables and not the model's intercept, which is statistically valid in all cases, hence why you subtract the `coef.true` value by 1. Next, you define a `coef.false` term as the opposite case: how many of the model's coefficients on the dependent variables are *not* statistically meaningful. Finally, you define a `model.rsq` value, which is the extracted R-squared model accuracy. You then put it all together in a data frame and define a final metric: `goodness`. This measure compares the ratio of statistically meaningful coefficients to the model's order:

```
model.order <- c(1,2,3,4,5,6)

coef.true <- c(
  table((summary(lm1)$coefficients[,4])<0.05) - 1
  ,table((summary(lm2)$coefficients[,4])<0.05) - 1
  ,table((summary(lm3)$coefficients[,4])<0.05)[2] - 1
  ,table((summary(lm4)$coefficients[,4])<0.05)[2] - 1
  ,table((summary(lm5)$coefficients[,4])<0.05)[2] - 1
  ,table((summary(lm6)$coefficients[,4])<0.05)[2] - 1

)

coef.false <- c(
  0
  ,0
  ,table((summary(lm3)$coefficients[,4])<0.05)[1]
  ,table((summary(lm4)$coefficients[,4])<0.05)[1]
  ,table((summary(lm5)$coefficients[,4])<0.05)[1]
  ,table((summary(lm6)$coefficients[,4])<0.05)[1]

)

model.rsq <- c(
  summary(lm1)$r.squared
  ,summary(lm2)$r.squared
  ,summary(lm3)$r.squared
  ,summary(lm4)$r.squared
  ,summary(lm5)$r.squared
  ,summary(lm6)$r.squared

)

model.comparison <- data.frame(model.order, model.rsq, coef.true, coef.false)
model.comparison$goodness <- (model.comparison$coef.true / model.comparison
$model.order)

model.comparison

##   model.order model.rsq coef.true coef.false  goodness
## 1           1 0.9223434         1          0 1.0000000
## 2           2 0.9982808         2          0 1.0000000
## 3           3 0.9983235         2          1 0.6666667
## 4           4 0.9984910         2          2 0.5000000
## 5           5 0.9992208         3          2 0.6000000
## 6           6 0.9993027         3          3 0.5000000
```

The result demonstrates that, although the model's R-squared accuracy might be increasing as the fit becomes more complex, the goodness of that fit goes down over time because the number of statistically meaningful coefficients compared to the total number of coefficients tends to go down. One way that you can statistically quantify this is to rank the associated elements you're interested in optimizing with the following:

```
model.comparison$rank <- sqrt(model.comparison$goodness^2 +
    model.comparison$model.rsq^2)
model.comparison
```

```
##   model.order model.rsq coef.true coef.false  goodness      rank
## 1           1 0.9223434         1          0 1.0000000 1.360411
## 2           2 0.9982808         2          0 1.0000000 1.412998
## 3           3 0.9983235         2          1 0.6666667 1.200456
## 4           4 0.9984910         2          2 0.5000000 1.116685
## 5           5 0.9992208         3          2 0.6000000 1.165522
## 6           6 0.9993027         3          3 0.5000000 1.117410
```

Now, you can see where the trade-off is best between model accuracy and goodness of fit. The model order with the highest rank in this case is a quadratic fit that has all of its coefficients that are statistically valid. Although the model fit for a third-degree polynomial is marginally better (almost unmeasurably so), the goodness of fit isn't great because we have a coefficient that is not statistically meaningful.

What we can say about this procedure is that we have an optimal model to choose that has the highest rank value. A model that has a lower R-squared and lower rank is underfit to the data. A model that has a higher R-squared and a lower rank is an overfit model to our data.

Logistic Regression

Thus far we've considered regression models in terms of taking some kind of numeric data to which we want to fit some kind of curve so that we can use it for predictive purposes. Linear regression takes some sort of numeric data and renders an equation like $y = mx + b$ out. Linear regression can also have multiple inputs and we could have an equation like $y = b + m_1x_1 + m_2x_2 + (...)$. Further, these types of numerical regression models can be turned into nonlinear cases such as $y = b + m_1x_1 + m_2x_1^2 + m_3x_1^3 + (...)$. All of these have their own use cases and are totally dependent on the data we're working with and how we strategize about the kind of accuracy for which we want to optimize.

All of these so far have ingested some numeric input and given us a numeric output. What if, instead, we wanted a "yes" or "no" outcome from our data? What if we were trying to do something like determine whether our input data was of a positive or negative result? In this case, we would be taking in continuous numeric data and getting some kind of discrete output. This is the basis for the classification end of our regression modeling. *Logistic regression* is a particular type of classification and relatively simple enough to be used as an introductory example. Logistic regression, in contrast to linear regression, finds the point at which the data goes from one kind of classification to another instead of trying to fit all the individual data points themselves.

The Motivation for Classification

Suppose that you are trying to diagnose patients to determine whether they have a malignant tumor. Let's look at the code and the resulting plot in Figure 4-7:

```
data <- data.frame(tumor.size <- c(1, 2, 3, 4, 5, 6, 7, 8, 9,
    20), malignant <- c(0, 0, 0, 0, 1, 1, 1, 1, 1, 1))

tumor.lm <- lm(malignant ~ tumor.size, data = data)

plot(y = data$malignant, x = data$tumor.size, main = "Tumor Malignancy by Size",
    ylab = "Type (0 = benign, 1 = cancerous)", xlab = "Tumor Size")

abline(a = coef(tumor.lm[1]), b = coef(tumor.lm[2]))

coef(tumor.lm)

## (Intercept)  tumor.size
##  0.20380952  0.06095238

summary(tumor.lm)$r.squared

## [1] 0.4063492
```

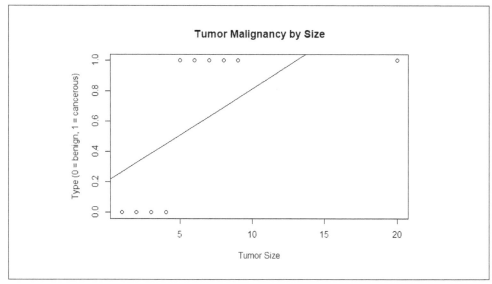

Figure 4-7. Fitting a linear regression line to binary data does not provide an accurate model

This code creates a dataset of tumor sizes from 1 to 20 and classifies whether they are malignant, with a benign or noncancerous tumor being classified as 0, and a malignant or cancerous tumor being labeled as 1. A naive instinct might be to slap a regression model on this data and see what the equation output is. With this approach, you would have an equation such as the following:

tumor malignancy = 0.061 × tumor size + 0.204

The poor fit of the R-squared at 0.406 suggests that we could obtain a more accurate model. Additionally, you should question the logical assessment of what it means to have a tumor that is 0.2 malignant when they are logged in the data as being either malignant or not with no room in between. This would also not make much sense with the mtcars dataset if we had something modeled against transmission type. What would a 0.2 transmission be if 0 was manual and 1 was an automatic?

We need to rethink this approach. Instead of fitting a normal mathematical function, we need to fit something called a *decision boundary* to the data.

The Decision Boundary

The decision boundary is simply a line in the sand of our data that says "anything on this side is classified as *X* and anything on the other side is classified as *Y*." Figure 4-8 revisits the plot of tumor sizes and whether they're malignant. You can clearly see that any tumor that's greater in size than 5 always seems to be malignant:

```
plot(y = data$malignant, x = data$tumor.size, main = "Tumor Malignancy by Size",
    ylab = "Type (0 = benign, 1 = cancerous)", xlab = "Tumor Size")
abline(v = 4.5)
```

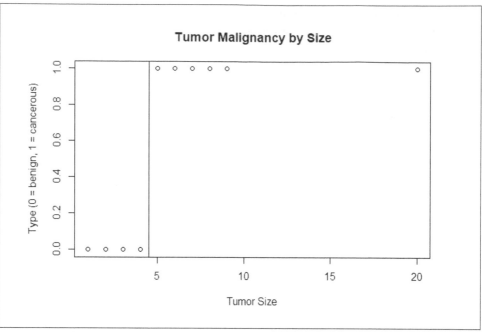

Figure 4-8. Plotting a decision boundary instead of a regression line classifies data less than about 4.5 as 0; data above that threshold is classified as 1

Logistic regression establishes the boundary against which you can classify data. The boundary in Figure 4-8 shows that any tumor size greater than 4.5 is malignant, whereas anything less than that is benign.

The Sigmoid Function

The way logistic regression (as well as many other types of classification algorithms) work is based on the mathematical underpinnings of the sigmoid function. The *sigmoid function* takes the following mathematical form:

$$h(x) = \frac{1}{1 + e^{-x}}$$

Figure 4-9 shows what the plot looks like:

```
e <- exp(1)
curve(1/(1 + e^-x), -10, 10, main = "The Sigmoid Function", xlab = "Input",
    ylab = "Probability")
```

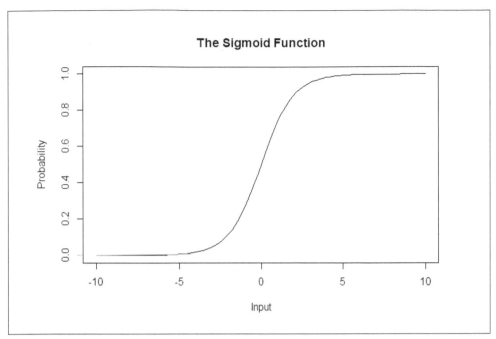

Figure 4-9. The sigmoid function is the basis for logistic regression

This function is used in logistic regression to classify data. On its own, the function takes in some numeric value that we are interested in and maps it to a probability between 0 and 1. We might be tempted to just plug in some of the values from our earlier example into the sigmoid function and see what the output is. If we did, like setting $x = 1$, for example, we would get $h(1) = 0.73$, or about a 73% chance a tumor is malignant if our input is 1. Yet our classification system is 0 for benign and 1 for malignant. The length = 1 input yields a result of 0.73, which is incorrect.

Instead, we need to pass a set of weighted parameters to the logistic regressor. Because we have only one dependent variable at the moment (keeping in mind that the y-axis for our classification output is not an input variable), we should expect to pass a function to our logistic regressor that has the form similar to the following:

$$g(\text{length}) = \theta_0 + \theta_1 \text{length}$$

A priori, we don't know what the weights are just yet. What we do want is for them to be chosen such that our $g(x)$ function, when passed to our sigmoid function, will give us a classification that looks reasonable to what we see in our data:

```
lengths <- c(1, 2, 3, 4, 5, 6, 7, 8, 9, 10)
t1 = -4.5
t2 = 1
g = t1 + t2 * lengths
s = 1/(1 + e^-g)
data.frame(lengths, g, s)

##    lengths    g            s
## 1        1 -3.5 0.02931223
## 2        2 -2.5 0.07585818
## 3        3 -1.5 0.18242552
## 4        4 -0.5 0.37754067
## 5        5  0.5 0.62245933
## 6        6  1.5 0.81757448
## 7        7  2.5 0.92414182
## 8        8  3.5 0.97068777
## 9        9  4.5 0.98901306
## 10      10  5.5 0.99592986
```

This code chunk takes the input tumor lengths, which range from 1 to 10, and picks two weights of $\theta_0 = 4.5$ and $\theta_0 = 1$. In practice, you would either need to experiment with picking values for the weights and seeing how the outputs react, or crunch them through an algorithm that gives you the answer. The preceding code provides the answer as an end result. They are then used as the weights for the function $g(x)$ that is then passed to the sigmoid. The table in the code presents the resultant classification of the data as s. A tumor of length 1, when passed through the input function $g(x)$, gives a result of –3.5. This value, when passed to the sigmoid function, yields a result that's pretty close to zero. This means that a tumor of length 1 has a very low probability of being malignant, as demonstrated in Figure 4-10:

```
plot(y = s, x = lengths, pch = 1, main = "Sigmoid Function Inputs and Rounding
Estimates",
     xlab = "Tumor Lengths", ylab = "Probability of Class 1 Typification")

points(y = round(s), x = lengths, pch = 3)
```

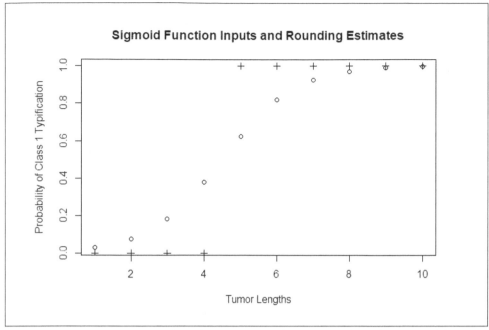

Figure 4-10. For a given input length, you can see the estimate from the sigmoid function in circles, and its rounded value in crosses

Figure 4-10 presents probabilities for tumor lengths being classified as malignant if the probability is 1.0 and benign if the probability is 0.0. The result is pretty close, but there's some error with it. You would get a much better picture if you simply round the values to the nearest whole number. The final result is a classification that looks exactly like the starting data.

We originally started with the input data being tumor length. The output of tumor type between benign, $y = 0$, and malignant, $y = 1$, was already given to us. The objective was to design a model that calculates the probability that a tumor is benign or malignant based on its length. We did this by starting with the equation $g(x) = \theta_0 + \theta_1 x$ and then finding the weights θ_0 and θ_1, which helped to get values out that, when passed through a sigmoid function, provided values that look about right for what we needed. What we get at the end of the day is a decision boundary at length = 4.5; any values above that are classified as 1, and any values below it are classified as 0.

The mechanisms by which classification algorithms like logistic regression work to determine those modeling weights are somewhat similar in scope to how simple linear regression weights are calculated. However, given that the goal of this text is to be introductory in nature, I'll refer you to the statistical appendix for linear regression. Logistic regression and many other machine learning algorithms work in a similar fashion, but diving too deep into the realm of algorithm optimization can get overly mathy and we would lose focus on the understanding and application of the machine learning ecosystem as a whole.

Binary Classification

Everything we've done so far in terms of classification has been on binary data: the tumor is either malignant or benign. Figure 4-11 looks at another example in which we determine the classes based on the data's distribution:

```
plot(iris$Sepal.Length ~ iris$Sepal.Width, main = "Iris Flower Sepal Length vs
Sepal Width",
    xlab = "Sepal Width", ylab = "Sepal Length")
```

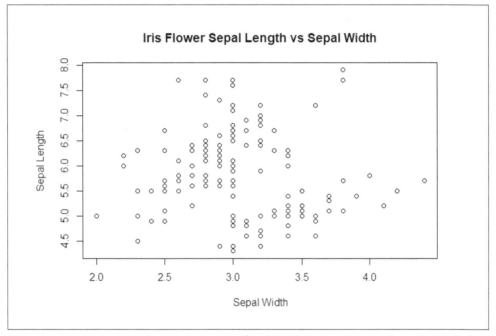

Figure 4-11. You can use logistic regression for data that is more spread out instead of being discrete in output

In Figure 4-11, there are a bunch of data points and what appears to be two different classes of plants. There looks to be a grouping of data points at the bottom of the plot that seem to be more separated than the others. You can fit a logistic regression model to this data and find the equation for the line that makes your decision boundary. Any points below that threshold will be classified as one type, and all the points above the line will be classified as another type.

This exercise uses a generalized linear model, given by the function glm(). Its usage is more flexible than that of the standard linear model function lm() in that you can use it for classification purposes:

```
iris.binary <- iris
iris.binary$binary <- as.numeric(iris[, 5] == "setosa")


iris.logistic <- glm(binary ~ Sepal.Width + Sepal.Length, data = iris.binary,
    family = "binomial")
iris.logistic

##
## Call:  glm(formula = binary ~ Sepal.Width + Sepal.Length,
##      family = "binomial", data = iris.binary)
##
## Coefficients:
##  (Intercept)   Sepal.Width  Sepal.Length
##        437.2         137.9        -163.4
##
## Degrees of Freedom: 149 Total (i.e. Null);  147 Residual
## Null Deviance:       191
## Residual Deviance: 2.706e-08    AIC: 6
```

The output from this method provides some coefficients and intercepts that don't look totally right. You need one extra step to calculate the slope and intercepts of the decision boundary this way. Recall for a moment how you used the sigmoid function $g(z) = 1/(1 + e\ z)$.

z is a function with the following form:

$$z = \theta_0 + \theta_1 x_1 + \theta_2 x_2$$

Because you want a value between 0 and 1 for binary classification, the classification is 1 when you have your sigmoid function $g(z) \geq 0.5$. That's only true when the function z that you pass it is itself greater than 0:

$$0 \leq \theta_0 + \theta_1 x_1 + \theta_2 x_2$$

You can rewrite this equation and solve for our x_2 value accordingly:

$$x_2 \geq \frac{-\theta_0}{\theta_2} + \frac{-\theta_1}{\theta_2} x1$$

This equation is the same form as a $y = b + mx$ line, where we can solve computationally for the slope and intercept to build out the function that determines the decision boundary:

$$\text{slope} = -x_1/x_2 = -137.9/163.4$$

$$\text{intercept} = -b/x_2 = -437.2/163.4$$

You can calculate this directly from the logistic model object:

```
slope.iris <- coef(iris.logistic)[2]/(-coef(iris.logistic)[3])
int.iris <- coef(iris.logistic)[1]/(-coef(iris.logistic)[3])

slope.iris

## Sepal.Width
##    0.8440957

int.iris

## (Intercept)
##    2.675511
```

You then can plot this over your data and see how the classes shake out, as illustrated in Figure 4-12:

```
iris.binary$binary[iris.binary$binary == 0] <- 2

plot(Sepal.Length ~ Sepal.Width, data = iris.binary, pch = (binary),
     main = "Iris Flower Sepal Length vs Sepal Width", xlab = "Sepal Width",
     ylab = "Sepal Length")

abline(a = int.iris, b = slope.iris)
```

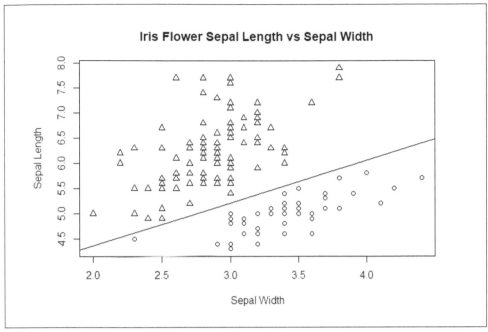

Figure 4-12. Splitting a distribution of data into two classes

You now have an equation that helps determine how to separate the species of iris flowers we have. Any flowers in the dataset that have a value below the line of $y = 2.68 + 0.844 \times$ (Sepal.Width) will be classified accordingly.

Multiclass Classification

If you want to find the splits in your data that define multiple classes and not just a binary classification, you need to use *multiclass classification*. This approach is slightly different in that you are basically applying the same binary classification scheme that you have been doing thus far, but you are comparing the class you're interested in versus everything else.

Figure 4-13 illustrates what a multiclass classification exercise might look like:

```
multi <- data.frame(x1 = c(0.03, 0.24, 0.21, 0, 0, 0.23, 0.6,
    0.64, 0.86, 0.77), x2 = c(0.07, 0.06, 0.19, 1.15, 0.95, 1,
    0.81, 0.64, 0.44, 0.74), lab = c(1, 1, 1, 2, 2, 2, 3, 3,
    3, 3))

plot(x2 ~ x1, pch = lab, cex = 2, data = multi,
    main = "Multi-Class Classification",
    xlab = "x", ylab = "y")
```

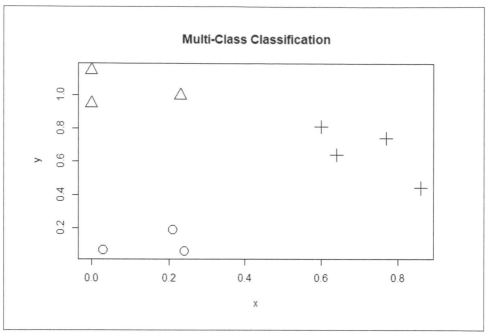

Figure 4-13. Multiclass data can be separated only by using a one-versus-many approach

There are three distinct classes of data, and you want to find some kind of lines that split them into their own categories, much like you did for the binary case. What this essentially boils down to is our simple binary test, but you change which group you're comparing against. This is called a "one-versus-all" or "one-versus-many" test, in which you test three cases—triangles-versus-rest, circles-versus-rest, and crosses-versus-rest, as depicted in Figure 4-14:

```
par(mfrow = c(1, 3))
multi$lab2 <- c(1, 1, 1, 4, 4, 4, 4, 4, 4, 4)
plot(x2 ~ x1, pch = lab2, cex = 2, data = multi,
    main = "Multi-Class Classification",
    xlab = "x", ylab = "y")

multi$lab3 <- c(4, 4, 4, 2, 2, 2, 4, 4, 4, 4)
plot(x2 ~ x1, pch = lab3, cex = 2, data = multi,
    main = "Multi-Class Classification",
    xlab = "x", ylab = "y")

multi$lab4 <- c(4, 4, 4, 4, 4, 4, 3, 3, 3, 3)
plot(x2 ~ x1, pch = lab4, cex = 2, data = multi,
    main = "Multi-Class Classification",
    xlab = "x", ylab = "y")
```

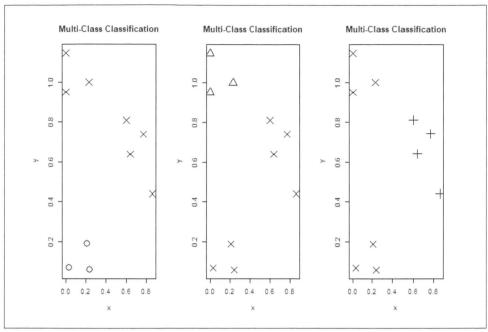

Figure 4-14. One-versus-many classification utilizes the same approach as standard classification but reclassifies other groups into one single group for comparison

In a one-versus-many classification approach, you use one decision boundary to classify data for one type or class versus all the other types or classes. You then do the same for the rest of the types or classes in the data until you have a number of decision boundaries that you can use to typify your data accordingly. So, for the example in Figure 4-14, you're computing (on the left plot) the circles versus the rest of the data, and then you compute the triangles versus the rest of the data (middle plot), and, finally, the crosses versus the rest of the data (right plot). By splitting a three-class problem into three, two-class problems, you can more easily find a single decision boundary for each plot and then combine those decision boundaries for a final model.

Here, you call upon the `nnet` library's function `multinom()`. You use this to pass a multinomial case that's basically the same as you've done for the simple binary case, but with three values instead of two. This methodology can be applied for more than three categories:

```
library(nnet)
multi.model <- multinom(lab ~ x2 + x1, data = multi, trace = F)
```

Notice that you have two lines to separate the three categories:

```
multi.model

## Call:
## multinom(formula = lab ~ x2 + x1, data = multi, trace = F)
##
## Coefficients:
##    (Intercept)        x2        x1
## 2    -12.47452  28.50805 -17.97523
## 3    -19.82927  12.95949  33.39610
##
## Residual Deviance: 0.0004050319
## AIC: 12.00041
```

Again, however, you need to do the special calculation for the slopes and intercepts of the decision boundaries based on the output of this model. You can apply the same math as earlier, but you need to apply it to each of the equations from the model. Then, you can plot the decision boundary lines, as illustrated in Figure 4-15:

```
multi.int.1 <- -coef(multi.model)[1]/coef(multi.model)[3]
multi.slope.1 <- -coef(multi.model)[5]/coef(multi.model)[3]

multi.int.2 <- -coef(multi.model)[2]/coef(multi.model)[4]
multi.slope.2 <- -coef(multi.model)[6]/coef(multi.model)[4]


plot(x2 ~ x1, pch = lab, cex = 2, data = multi,
    main = "Multi-Class Classification",
    xlab = "x", ylab = "y")
abline(multi.int.1, multi.slope.1)
abline(multi.int.2, multi.slope.2)
```

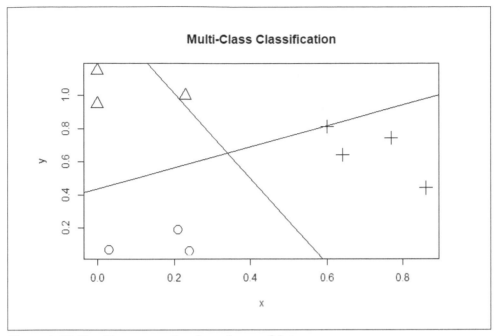

Figure 4-15. Two lines separating three classes of data

Logistic Regression with Caret

The `caret` package makes doing logistic regression problems very easy for more complex examples than what we have been doing thus far. Using `caret` is fairly straightforward, though for some particular machine learning methods, some optimizations and tunings might be warranted to achieve the best results possible. Following is an example of how you can perform an operation with `caret`:

```
library(caret)

data("GermanCredit")

Train <- createDataPartition(GermanCredit$Class, p = 0.6, list = FALSE)
training <- GermanCredit[Train, ]
testing <- GermanCredit[-Train, ]

mod_fit <- train(Class ~ Age + ForeignWorker + Property.RealEstate +
    Housing.Own + CreditHistory.Critical, data = training, method = "glm",
    family = "binomial")


predictions <- predict(mod_fit, testing[, -10])
table(predictions, testing[, 10])
```

```
##
## predictions Bad Good
##         Bad   9    8
##         Good 111  272
```

This simple example uses data from the GermanCredit dataset and shows how you can build a confusion matrix from a caret training object. In this case, the fit doesn't seem super great, because about 50% of the data seems to be classified incorrectly. Although caret offers some great ways to tune whatever particular machine learning method you are interested in, it's also quite flexible at changing machine learning methods. By simply editing the method option, you can specify one of the other 12 logistic regression algorithms to pass to the model, as shown here:

```
mod_fit <- train(Class ~ Age + ForeignWorker + Property.RealEstate +
    Housing.Own + CreditHistory.Critical, data = training,
    method = "LogitBoost",
    family = "binomial")

predictions <- predict(mod_fit, testing[, -10])
table(predictions, testing[, 10])

##
## predictions Bad Good
##         Bad   7   15
##         Good 113  265
```

Summary

In this chapter, we looked at a couple different ways to build basic models between simple linear regression and logistic regression.

Linear Regression

Regression comes in two forms: standard linear regression, which you might have encountered early on in your mathematics classes, and logistic regression, which is very different. R can create a linear model with ease by using the lm() function. In tandem with R's formula operator, ~, you can build a simple $y = mx + b$ regression equation by doing something like lm(y~x). From this linear model object, you can extract a wealth of information regarding coefficients, statistical validity, and accuracy. You can do this by using the summary() function, which can tell you how statistically valid each coefficient in your model is. For those that aren't statistically useful, you can safely remove them from your model.

Regression models can be more advanced by having more features. You can model behavior like fuel efficiency as a function of a vehicle's weight, but you can also incorporate more things into your model, such as a vehicle's transmission type, how many cylinders its engine might have, and so forth. Multivariate regression modeling in R follows the same practice as single-feature regression. The only difference is that there are more features listed in the `summary()` view of your model.

However, simply adding more features to a model doesn't make it more accurate by default. You might need to employ techniques like regularization, which takes a dataset that has lots of features and reduces the impact of those that aren't statistically as important as others. This can help you to simplify your model drastically and boost accuracy assessments, as well.

Sometimes, there might be nonlinear relationships in the data that require polynomial fits. A regular linear model is of the form $y = b + m_1x_1 + m_2x_2 + (\ldots)$, whereas a polynomial model might have the form $y = m_1x_1^2 + m_2x_1 + m_3x_2^2 + m_4x_2 + (\ldots)$. You can fit polynomial behavior to your models by passing a `poly()` function to the `lm()` function; for example, `lm(y~poly(x,2))`. This creates a quadratic relationship in the data. It's important to not go too crazy with polynomial degrees, however, because you run the risk of fitting your data so tightly that any new data that comes in might have high error estimates that aren't true to form.

Logistic Regression

In machine learning, there are standard regression techniques that estimate continuous values like numbers, and classification techniques that estimate discrete values like data types. In a lot of cases, the data can have discrete values like a flower's species. If you try the standard linear regression techniques on these datasets, you'll end up with very disingenuous relationships in your data that are better suited for classification schemes.

Logistic regression is a classification method that finds a boundary that separates data into discrete classes. It does this by passing the data through a sigmoid function that maps the actual value of the data to a binary 1 or 0 case. That result is then passed through another equation that yields weights to assign probabilities to the data. You can use this to determine how likely a given data point is of a certain class.

You can also use logistic regression to draw decision boundaries in your data. A decision boundary is a line that doesn't necessarily fit the data in a standard (x, y) plot, but fits gaps in the data to separate them into specific classes. In the case of data for which you have two classes, you would have one line that splits your data into class 1 and class 2.

In the case of multiple classes, you treat each class as a one-versus-many approach. If you have three classes, you focus on one and group the other two together and find the decision boundary that separates them, and then move on to the next class. At the end, you should have series of decision boundaries that separate the data into zones. Any data in a particular zone is classified the same as the data points in that zone.

## CHAPTER 5

Neural Networks in a Nutshell

In Chapter 2, we briefly touched on the topic of neural networks in our exploration of the machine learning landscape. A neural network is a set of equations that we use to calculate an outcome. They aren't so scary if we think of them as a brain made out of computer code. In some cases, this is closer to reality than we should expect from such a cartoony example. Depending on the number of features we have in our data, the neural network almost becomes a "black box." In principle, we can display the equations that make up a neural network, but at a certain level, the amount of information becomes too cumbersome to intuit easily.

Neural networks are used far and wide in industry largely due to their accuracy. Sometimes, there are trade-offs between having a highly accurate model, but slow computation speeds, however. Therefore, it's best to try multiple models and use neural networks only if they work for your particular dataset.

Single-Layer Neural Networks

In Chapter 2, we looked at the development of an AND gate. An AND gate follows logic like this:

```
x1 <- c(0, 0, 1, 1)
x2 <- c(0, 1, 0, 1)
logic <- data.frame(x1, x2)
logic$AND <- as.numeric(x1 & x2)
logic

##   x1 x2 AND
## 1  0  0   0
## 2  0  1   0
## 3  1  0   0
## 4  1  1   1
```

If you have two 1 inputs (both TRUE), your output is 1 (TRUE). However, if either of them, or both, are 0 (FALSE), your output is also 0 (FALSE). This computation is somewhat similar to our analysis of logistic regression. In Chapter 4, we covered how the sigmoid function works. Recall that the sigmoid function is given by $g(z) = f/(1 + e z)$, and that z is a function of the form $z = \theta_0 + \theta_1 x_1 + \theta_2 x_2$.

For the logic gate, all you need to do is pick and choose weights θ_0, θ_1, θ_2 so that when $x_1 = 1$ and $x_2 = 1$, the result of z when you pass it through the sigmoid function $g(z)$ is also 1. Previously, you picked weights of $\theta_0 = 20$, $\theta_1 = 15$, and $\theta_2 = 17$ to satisfy the equation. The way the neural network goes about computing those weights is an even more mathy process, but it follows the same sort of logic for what we used in logistic regression.

Neural networks come in many different flavors, but the most popular ones stem from single or multilayered neural networks. So far, you've seen an example of a single-layer network, for which we take some input (1,0), process it through a sigmoid function, and get some output (0). You can, in fact, chain together these computational steps to form more interconnected and complicated models by taking the output and passing it into futher computational layers.

Figure 5-1 presents an example of the AND gate with R code this time:

```
library(neuralnet)

set.seed(123)
AND <- c(rep(0, 3), 1)
binary.data <- data.frame(expand.grid(c(0, 1), c(0, 1)), AND)
net <- neuralnet(AND ~ Var1 + Var2, binary.data, hidden = 0,
    err.fct = "ce", linear.output = FALSE)
plot(net, rep = "best")
```

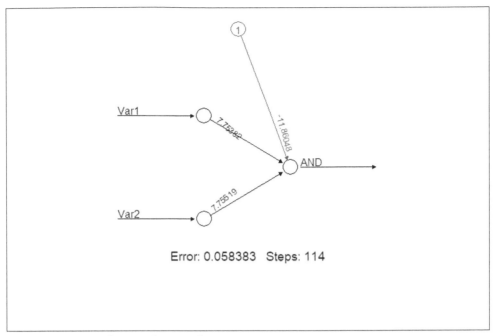

Figure 5-1. A simple neural network

Building a Simple Neural Network by Using R

Before we jump into the math, let's first break down the visualization presented in Figure 5-1, a diagram of a neural network that's about as simple as it can get. There is one input layer (the empty circles on the left) and one output layer (the empty circle on the right). Often, there is another vertical layer of circles that indicates a compute layer. In this case, the output layer is the compute layer. The numbers on the lines indicate the computationally crunched best weights to use for the model. The number attached to the "1" in the circle at the top is the weight from the *bias node*. The bias node is just the additive constant for the now-familiar sigmoid function you used in the logistic regression examples. So, in a sense, this is just a different way to represent a logistic regression analysis at a neural network's simplest form. The end result of which is a classification scheme for the data that has labels 1 or 0.

In R, there's really only one neural network library that has built-in functionality for plotting neural networks. In practice, most of the time plotting neural networks is more complicated than it's worth, as we will demonstrate later. In complex modeling scenarios, neural network diagrams and mathematics become so cumbersome that the model itself more or less becomes a trained black box. If your manager were to ask you to explain the math behind a complex neural network model, you might need to block out an entire afternoon and find the largest whiteboard in the building.

The `neuralnet` library has built-in plotting functionality, however, and in the previous case, you are plotting the neural network that has been determined to have the lowest error in this case. The number of steps are the number of iterations that have gone on in the background to tune the particular output for its lowest error.

The code shown in Figure 5-1 passes a similar table of data from `binary.data` into the `neuralnet()` function from the package of the same name. The result you get out would be an equation that has weights $\theta_0 = 11.86048$, $\theta_1 = 7.75382$, and $\theta_2 = 7.75519$.

So, if your boss is truly eager to see what the status of your neural network modeling procedure is, you would be delighted and can say that you've finished and have the model ready to go. If your boss asks for details on how exactly the thing works, you can say that it takes in two inputs Var_1 and Var_2, and inputs them into the equation:

$$z = -11.96048 + 7.75382\,Var_1 + 7.75382\,Var_2$$

you then pass that equation through a sigmoid function $g(z) = 1/(1 + e^{-z})$ and get an output. So the entire process would look like this:

$$AND = \frac{1}{1 + e^{-(-11.96048 + 7.75382 * Var1 + 7.75382 * Var2)}}$$

You can check the `neuralnet()` function's output by using the `prediction()` function:

```
prediction(net)

## Data Error:  0;

## $rep1
##    Var1 Var2                  AND
## 1    0    0 0.000007064115737
## 2    1    0 0.016196147483124
## 3    0    1 0.016217878405446
## 4    1    1 0.974631032550725
##
## $data
##    Var1 Var2 AND
## 1    0    0   0
## 2    1    0   0
## 3    0    1   0
## 4    1    1   1
```

In the first table are the input variables and what the neural network thinks the answer is. As you can see, the answers are pretty close to what they should be, as given by the table below it. So far, you have successfully performed a neural network model with a single layer. That is, all of the inputs went into a single processing point as shown in Figure 5-1. These processing points are almost always sigmoid functions, but in some rare instances, they can be passed through a hyperbolic tan function, $\tanh(x)$, to achieve a similar result.

Multiple Compute Outputs

As alluded to earlier, neural networks can take multiple inputs and provide multiple outputs. If, for example, you have two functions that you want to model via neural networks, you can use R's formula operator ~ and the + operator to simply add another response to the lefthand side of the equation during modeling, as shown in Figure 5-2:

```
set.seed(123)
AND <- c(rep(0, 7), 1)
OR <- c(0, rep(1, 7))
binary.data <- data.frame(expand.grid(c(0, 1), c(0, 1), c(0,
    1)), AND, OR)
net <- neuralnet(AND + OR ~ Var1 + Var2 + Var3, binary.data,
    hidden = 0, err.fct = "ce", linear.output = FALSE)
plot(net, rep = "best")
```

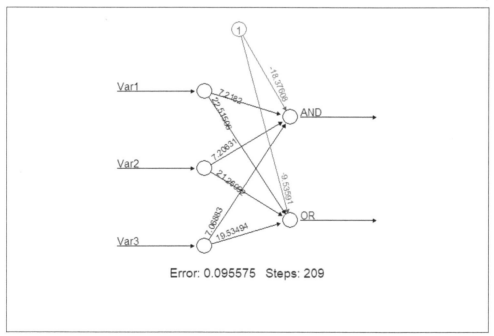

Figure 5-2. Neural networks can be more complex than logistic regression in terms of multiple compute outputs

We can model our AND and OR functions with two equations given by the outputs in Figure 5-2:

$$\text{AND} = 19.4 + 7.5 \times \text{Var1} + 7.6 \times \text{Var2} + 7.6 \times \text{Var3}$$
$$\text{OR} = 10.3 + 22.3 \times \text{Var1} + 21.8 \times \text{Var2} + 21.9 \times \text{Var3}$$

We can see our output in the same way as before with just one function:

```
prediction(net)

## Data Error:  0;

## $rep1
##   Var1 Var2 Var3                 AND                OR
## 1    0    0    0 0.00000001045614851 0.00007220621224
## 2    1    0    0 0.00001426236484049 0.99999769205959
## 3    0    1    0 0.00001409371095155 0.99999191105328
## 4    1    1    0 0.01886199255844006 1.00000000000000
## 5    0    0    1 0.00001228339436300 0.99995455791699
## 6    1    0    1 0.01647909336278272 0.99999999999999
## 7    0    1    1 0.01628739761101993 0.99999999999997
## 8    1    1    1 0.95759917455105847 1.00000000000000
##
## $data
##   Var1 Var2 Var3 AND OR
## 1    0    0    0   0  0
## 2    1    0    0   0  1
## 3    0    1    0   0  1
## 4    1    1    0   0  1
## 5    0    0    1   0  1
## 6    1    0    1   0  1
## 7    0    1    1   0  1
## 8    1    1    1   1  1
```

The neural networks seem to be performing quite nicely!

Hidden Compute Nodes

So far, you have been building neural networks that have no hidden layers. That is to say, the compute layer is the same as the output layer. The neural network we computed in Figure 5-3 comprised zero layers and one output layer. Here, we show you how adding one hidden layer of computation can help increase the model's accuracy.

Neural networks use a shorthand notation for defining their architecture, in which we note the number of input nodes, followed by a colon, the number of compute nodes in the hidden layer, another colon, and then the number of output nodes. The architecture of the neural network we built in Figure 5-3 was 3:0:1.

An easier way to illustrate this is by diagramming a neural network (see Figure 5-3) that has three inputs, one hidden layer, and one output layer for a 3:1:1 neural network architecture:

```
set.seed(123)
AND <- c(rep(0, 7), 1)
binary.data <- data.frame(expand.grid(c(0, 1), c(0, 1), c(0,
    1)), AND, OR)
net <- neuralnet(AND ~ Var1 + Var2 + Var3, binary.data, hidden = 1,
    err.fct = "ce", linear.output = FALSE)
plot(net, rep = "best")
```

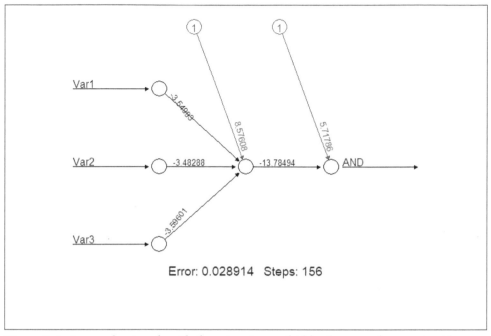

Error: 0.028914 Steps: 156

Figure 5-3. A neural network with three inputs, one hidden layer, and one output layer (3:1:1)

In this case, we have inserted a computation step before the output. Walking through the diagram from left to right, there are three inputs for a logic gate. These are crunched into a logistic regression function in the middle, hidden layer. The resultant equation is then pumped out to the compute layer for us to use for our AND function. The math would look something like this:

$$H1 = 8.57 + 3.6 \times \text{Var1} - 3.5 \times \text{Var2} - 3.6 \times \text{Var3}$$

Which we would then pass through a logistic regression function:

$$g(H\_1) = \frac{1}{1 + e^{-(8.57 + 3.6\text{Var1} - 3.5\text{Var2} - 3.6\text{Var3})}}$$

Next, we take *that* output and put it through *another* logistic regression node using the weights calculated on the output node:

$$AND = 5.72 - 13.79 \times g(H_1)$$

One major advantage of using a hidden layer with some hidden compute nodes is that it makes the neural network more accurate. However, the more complex you make a neural network model, the slower it will be and the more difficult it will be to simply explain it with easy-to-intuit equations. More hidden compute layers also means that you run the risk of overfitting your model, such as you've seen already with traditional regression modeling systems.

Although the numbers tied to the weights of each compute node shown in Figure 5-4 are now becoming pretty illegible, the main takeaway here is the error and number of computation steps. In this case, the error has gone down a little bit from 0.033 to 0.027 from the last model, but you've also reduced the number of computational steps to get that accuracy from 143 to 61. So, not only have you increased the accuracy, but you've made the model computation quicker at the same time. Figure 5-4 also shows another hidden computation node added to the single hidden layer, just before the output layer:

```
set.seed(123)

net2 <- neuralnet(AND ~ Var1 + Var2 + Var3, binary.data, hidden = 2,
    err.fct = "ce", linear.output = FALSE)

plot(net2, rep = "best")
```

Mathematically, this can be represented as two logistic regression equations being fed into a final logistic regression equation for our resultant output:

$$f_1 = 13.64 + 13.97 * Var1 + 14.9 * Var2 + 14.27 * Var3$$
$$f_2 = -7.95 + 3.24 * Var1 + 3.15 * Var2 + 3.29 * Var3$$
$$f_3 = -5.83 - 1.94 * f_1 + 14.09 * f_2$$
$$AND = g(f_3) = \frac{1}{1 + e^{-\left(-5.83 - 1.94 * f_1 + 14.09 * f_2\right)}}$$

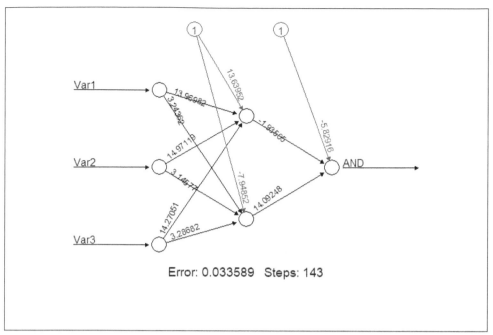

Figure 5-4. Visualized here is a 3:4:1 neural network architecture

The equations are becoming more and more complicated with each increase in the number of hidden compute nodes. The error with two nodes went up slightly from 0.29 to 0.33, but the number of iteration steps the model took to minimize that error was a little bit better in that it went down from 156 to 143. What happens if you turn the number of compute nodes even higher? Figures 5-5 and 5-6 illustrate this.

```
set.seed(123)

net4 <- neuralnet(AND ~ Var1 + Var2 + Var3, binary.data, hidden = 4,
    err.fct = "ce", linear.output = FALSE)
net8 <- neuralnet(AND ~ Var1 + Var2 + Var3, binary.data, hidden = 8,
    err.fct = "ce", linear.output = FALSE)

plot(net4, rep = "best")

plot(net8, rep = "best")
```

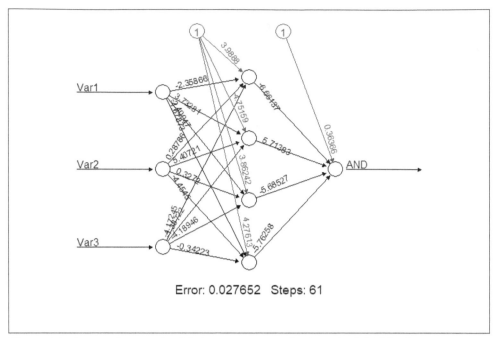

Figure 5-5. A neural network with four compute nodes in a single hidden layer

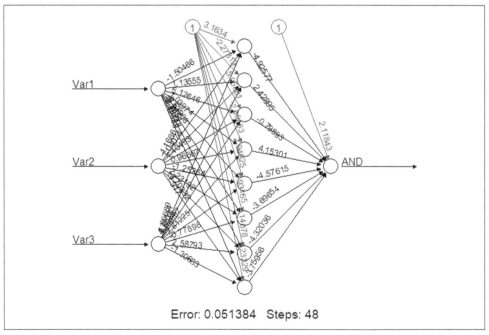

Figure 5-6. An overfitting 3:8:1 neural network model

The code in Figures 5-5 and 5-6 uses the same neural network modeling scenario, but the number of hidden computation nodes are increased first to four, and then to eight. The neural network with four hidden computation nodes had a better level of error (just slightly) than the network with only a single hidden node. The error in that case went down from 0.29 to 0.28, but the number of steps went down dramatically from 156 to 58. Quite an improvement! However, a neural network with eight hidden computation layers might have crossed into overfitting territory. In that network, error went from 0.29 to 0.34, even though the number of steps went from 156 to 51.

You can apply the same methodology with multiple outputs, as well, although the plot itself begins to become an unreadable mess at some point, as Figure 5-7 demonstrates:

```
set.seed(123)
net <- neuralnet(AND + OR ~ Var1 + Var2 + Var3, binary.data,
    hidden = 6, err.fct = "ce", linear.output = FALSE)
plot(net, rep = "best")
```

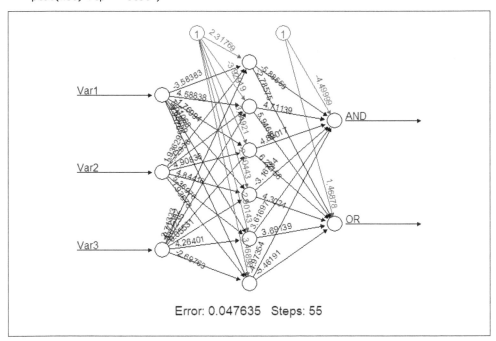

Figure 5-7. We can also design neural networks to have multiple compute outputs, while still having multiple compute nodes in the hidden layer

Multilayer Neural Networks

All the neural networks thus far that we've played around with have had an architecture that has one input layer, one or zero hidden layers (or compute layers), and one output layer.

We've used 1:1:1 or 1:0:1 neural networks for some classification schemes already. In those examples, we were trying to model classifications based on the AND and OR logic gate functions:

```
x1 <- c(0, 0, 1, 1)
x2 <- c(0, 1, 0, 1)
logic <- data.frame(x1, x2)
logic$AND <- as.numeric(x1 & x2)
logic$OR <- as.numeric(x1 | x2)
logic

##   x1 x2 AND OR
## 1  0  0   0  0
## 2  0  1   0  1
## 3  1  0   0  1
## 4  1  1   1  1
```

As Figure 5-8 demonstrates, we can represent this table as two plots, one of which shows the input values and colors those according to the type of logic gate output we use:

```
logic$AND <- as.numeric(x1 & x2) + 1
logic$OR <- as.numeric(x1 | x2) + 1

par(mfrow = c(2, 1))

plot(x = logic$x1, y = logic$x2, pch = logic$AND, cex = 2,
    main = "Simple Classification of Two Types",
    xlab = "x", ylab = "y", xlim = c(-0.5, 1.5), ylim = c(-0.5,
        1.5))

plot(x = logic$x1, y = logic$x2, pch = logic$OR, cex = 2,
    main = "Simple Classification of Two Types",
    xlab = "x", ylab = "y", xlim = c(-0.5, 1.5), ylim = c(-0.5,
        1.5))
```

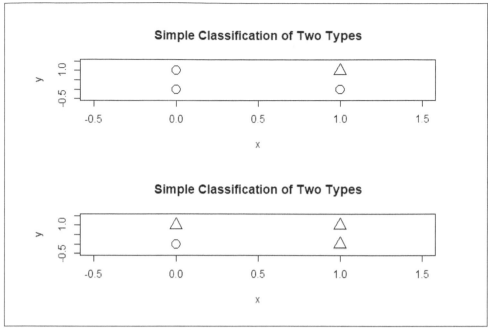

Figure 5-8. In these two cases of classification, we can separate the two classes by drawing a straight line decision boundary

These plots use triangles to signify when outputs are 1 (or TRUE), and circles for which the outputs are 0 (or FALSE). In our discussion on logistic regression, we were basically solving for some kind of line that would separate this data into red dots on one side and black dots on the other. Recall that this separating line is called a *decision boundary* and had always been a straight line. However, we can't use a straight line to try to classify more complicated logic gates like an XOR or XNOR.

In tabular form, as we've seen with the AND and OR functions, the XOR and XNOR functions take inputs of x1, x2, and give us a numeric output in much the same way, as demonstrated in Figure 5-9:

```
x1 <- c(0, 0, 1, 1)
x2 <- c(0, 1, 0, 1)
logic <- data.frame(x1, x2)
logic$AND <- as.numeric(x1 & x2)
logic$OR <- as.numeric(x1 | x2)
logic$XOR <- as.numeric(xor(x1, x2))
logic$XNOR <- as.numeric(x1 == x2)
logic

##   x1 x2 AND OR XOR XNOR
## 1  0  0   0  0   0    1
## 2  0  1   0  1   1    0
```

```
## 3  1  0    0  1    1    0
## 4  1  1    1  1    0    1

logic$XOR <- as.numeric(xor(x1, x2)) + 1
logic$XNOR <- as.numeric(x1 == x2) + 1

par(mfrow = c(2, 1))

plot(x = logic$x1, y = logic$x2, pch = logic$XOR, cex = 2, main = "Non-Linear
Classification of Two Types",
    xlab = "x", ylab = "y", xlim = c(-0.5, 1.5), ylim = c(-0.5,
        1.5))

plot(x = logic$x1, y = logic$x2, pch = logic$XNOR, cex = 2, main = "Non-Linear
Classification of Two Types",
    xlab = "x", ylab = "y", xlim = c(-0.5, 1.5), ylim = c(-0.5,
        1.5))
```

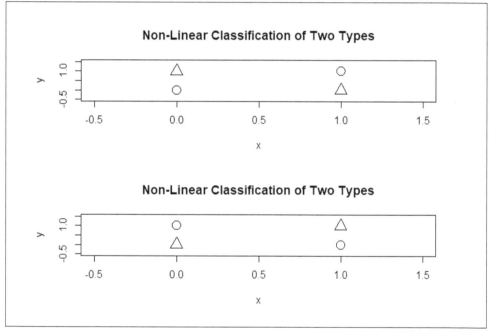

Figure 5-9. In these two cases, no one straight line can separate the two classes; however, multiple straight lines combined together can form a curve that you can use as a nonlinear decision boundary to separate the classes of data

There's no single straight line that can separate red and black dots on the plots in Figure 5-9. If you try to plot a very simple neural network with no hidden layers for an XOR classification, the results aren't especially gratifying, as illustrated in Figure 5-10:

```
logic$XOR <- as.numeric(xor(x1, x2))

set.seed(123)
net.xor <- neuralnet(XOR ~ x1 + x2, logic, hidden = 0, err.fct = "ce",
    linear.output = FALSE)
prediction(net.xor)

## Data Error:  0;

## $rep1
##    x1 x2        XOR
## 1  0  0 0.4870312778
## 2  1  0 0.4970850626
## 3  0  1 0.4980804563
## 4  1  1 0.5081363898
##
## $data
##    x1 x2 XOR
## 1  0  0  0
## 2  1  0  1
## 3  0  1  1
## 4  1  1  0

plot(net.xor, rep = "best")
```

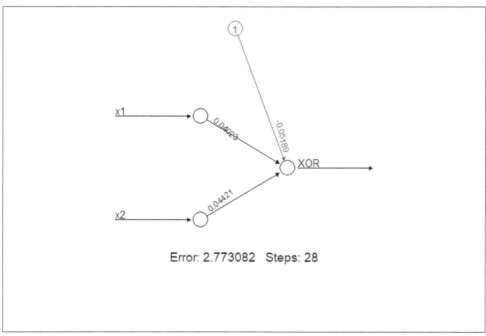

Figure 5-10. Computing a nonlinear output with a single hidden layer (in this case, the hidden layer is the computation layer) produces huge errors

Trying to use a neural network with no hidden layers will result in a huge error. Looking at the output from the `prediction()` function, you can see that the neural network thinks that for a given scenario, such as `xor(0,0)`, the answer is 0.5 ± 2.77. Having an error that is much higher than the level of granularity that you're trying to find the answer for indicates that this isn't the best method for you to use.

Instead of the traditional approach of using one or zero hidden layers, which provide a straight line decision boundary that is being used, you must rely on nonlinear decision boundaries, or curves, to separate classes of data. By adding more hidden layers to your neural networks, you add more logistic regression decision boundaries as straight lines. From these added lines, you can draw a convex decision boundary that enables nonlinearity. For this, you must rely on a class of neural networks called *multilayer perceptrons*, or MLPs.

One quick-and-dirty way of using an MLP in this case would be to use the inputs *x*1 and *x*2 to get the outputs of the AND and OR functions. You then can feed those outputs as individual inputs into a single-layer neural network, as illustrated in Figure 5-11:

```
set.seed(123)
and.net <- neuralnet(AND ~ x1 + x2, logic, hidden = 2, err.fct = "ce",
    linear.output = FALSE)
and.result <- data.frame(prediction(and.net)$rep1)

## Data Error:  0;

or.net <- neuralnet(OR ~ x1 + x2, logic, hidden = 2, err.fct = "ce",
    linear.output = FALSE)
or.result <- data.frame(prediction(or.net)$rep1)

## Data Error:  0;

as.numeric(xor(round(and.result$AND), round(or.result$OR)))

## [1] 0 1 1 0

xor.data <- data.frame(and.result$AND, or.result$OR,
as.numeric(xor(round(and.result$AND),
    round(or.result$OR))))
names(xor.data) <- c("AND", "OR", "XOR")

xor.net <- neuralnet(XOR ~ AND + OR, data = xor.data, hidden = 0,
    err.fct = "ce", linear.output = FALSE)

prediction(xor.net)

## Data Error:  0;

## $rep1
##               AND           OR           XOR
## 1 0.000175498243 0.01115157179 0.013427052868
## 2 0.002185508146 0.99537740097 0.993710672686
## 3 0.008091828479 0.99566427543 0.993306664121
```

```
## 4 0.985343384090 0.99806091842 0.003024047907
##
## $data
##                 AND            OR XOR
## 1 0.000175498243 0.01115157179   0
## 2 0.002185508146 0.99537740097   1
## 3 0.008091828479 0.99566427543   1
## 4 0.985343384090 0.99806091842   0
```

```
plot(xor.net, rep = "best")
```

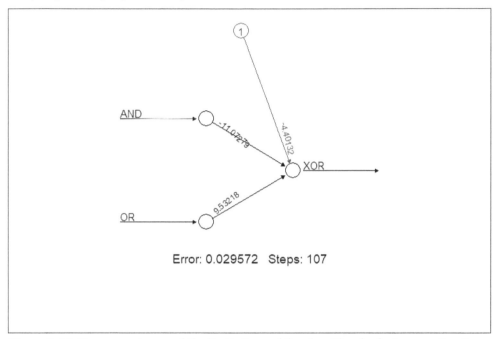

Figure 5-11. You can get around the limitations of the algorithm by first computing the single layer and then passing the results into another single layer of computation to emulate a multilayer neural network

An MLP is exactly what its name implies. A *perceptron* is a particular type of neural network that involves a specific way of how it calculates the weights and errors, known as a *feed-forward* neural network. By taking that principle and adding multiple hidden layers, we make it compatible with nonlinear data like the kind we are dealing with in an XOR gate.

Neural Networks for Regression

We've looked at some exhaustive examples that demonstrate how you can use neural networks to build systems like AND and OR gates, the outputs of which you can then combine to form stuff like XOR gates. Neural networks are decent at modeling simple functions but when you chain them together, you sometimes need to rely on more complex phenomena like MLPs.

You can use neural networks for standard machine learning problems like regression and classification, too. To gently walk through using neural networks for regression, let's look at Figure 5-12, which depicts a simple example with a familiar linear regression case so we have a good baseline of understanding. For this example, let's use the BostonHousing dataset from the mlbench library:

```
library(mlbench)
data(BostonHousing)

lm.fit <- lm(medv ~ ., data = BostonHousing)

lm.predict <- predict(lm.fit)

plot(BostonHousing$medv, lm.predict, main = "Linear regression predictions vs
actual",
    xlab = "Actual", ylab = "Prediction")
```

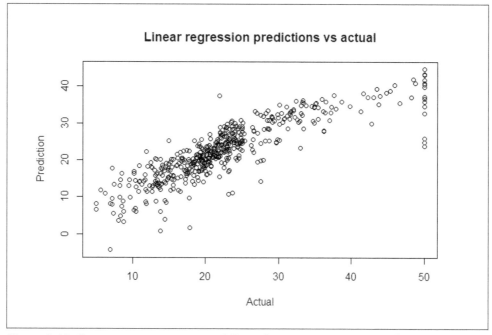

Figure 5-12. One way to measure a model's performance is to compare the outputs from its predictions to what they actually are

This creates a linear model of medv, the median value of owner-occupied homes in thousands of dollars. Next, the predict() function iterates over all the entries in the dataset using the model you created, and stores the predictions. The predictions are then plotted versus the actual values. In an ideal case of a perfect model, the resultant plot would be a perfectly linear relationship of $y = x$.

So how does neural network regression compare? Figure 5-13 shows how:

```
library(nnet)

nnet.fit1 <- nnet(medv ~ ., data = BostonHousing, size = 2)

## # weights:  31
## initial  value 283985.903126
## final  value 277329.140000
## converged

nnet.predict1 <- predict(nnet.fit1)

plot(BostonHousing$medv, nnet.predict1, main = "Neural network predictions vs
actual",
    xlab = "Actual", ylab = "Prediction")
```

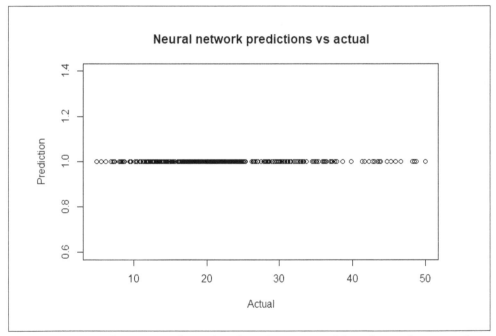

Figure 5-13. Something to watch out for when changing models is the need to normalize data first

According to our fit of a neural network with two hidden nodes in one hidden computation layer, the output is actually rather terrible. This should warrant some deeper investigation. Let's take a look at the response:

```
summary(BostonHousing$medv)
```

```
##     Min.  1st Qu.   Median     Mean  3rd Qu.      Max.
##   5.00000 17.02500 21.20000 22.53281 25.00000 50.00000
```

The range for the response is from 5 to 50. Neural networks aren't very good at using numbers that vary so greatly, so you need to employ a technique known as *feature scaling*. Feature scaling is the practice of normalizing your data to values between 0 and 1 so that you can feed it into certain machine learning models for more accurate outcomes. In this case, you want to divide your response by 50 so as to normalize the data:

```
summary(BostonHousing$medv/50)
```

```
##      Min.   1st Qu.    Median      Mean   3rd Qu.       Max.
## 0.1000000 0.3405000 0.4240000 0.4506561 0.5000000 1.0000000
```

Now, you have a response that has a minimum of 0.1 and a maximum of 1. Figure 5-14 shows how this affects the neural network modeling:

```
nnet.fit2 <- nnet(medv/50 ~ ., data = BostonHousing, size = 2,
    maxit = 1000, trace = FALSE)

nnet.predict2 <- predict(nnet.fit2) * 50

plot(BostonHousing$medv, nnet.predict2, main = "Neural network predictions vs
    actual with normalized response inputs",
    xlab = "Actual", ylab = "Prediction")
```

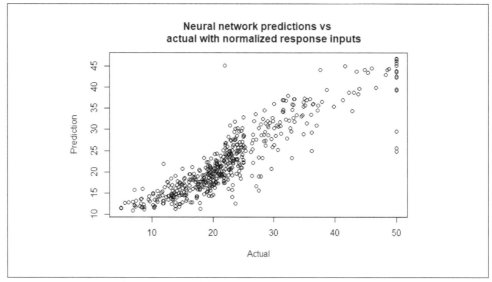

Figure 5-14. A neural network model output with properly normalized inputs

This plot looks a bit better than what you had before, but it's even better to quantify the difference between the two modeling scenarios. You can do this by looking at the mean squared errors:

```
mean((lm.predict - BostonHousing$medv)^2)
## [1] 21.89483118
mean((nnet.predict2 - BostonHousing$medv)^2)
## [1] 16.12870045
```

The total error for the linear model is just about 22, whereas the total error for the regression example done with a neural network has improved to about 16.

Alternatively, you can use the powerful R tool caret to better tune your model. By invoking caret, you can pass in some tuning parameters and sampling techniques to get a better estimate of error and more accurate results, as shown here:

```
library(caret)

mygrid <- expand.grid(.decay = c(0.5, 0.1), .size = c(4, 5, 6))
nnetfit <- train(medv/50 ~ ., data = BostonHousing, method = "nnet",
    maxit = 1000, tuneGrid = mygrid, trace = F)
print(nnetfit)

## Neural Network
##
## 506 samples
##   13 predictor
##
## No preprocessing
## Resampling: Bootstrapped (25 reps)
## Summary of sample sizes: 506, 506, 506, 506, 506, 506, ...
## Resampling results across tuning parameters:
##
##   decay  size  RMSE         Rsquared      MAE
##   0.1    4     0.08129182420  0.8053225697  0.05665268091
##   0.1    5     0.08118237926  0.8066818139  0.05718789316
##   0.1    6     0.07994531428  0.8111942947  0.05635562702
##   0.5    4     0.08929967985  0.7751011554  0.06278120999
##   0.5    5     0.08787920992  0.7803463408  0.06158346796
##   0.5    6     0.08686936074  0.7847302615  0.06107504984
##
## RMSE was used to select the optimal model using  the smallest value.
## The final values used for the model were size = 6 and decay = 0.1.
```

The best error estimate from this case has size 6, which means six nodes in the one hidden layer of the network, and a parameter decay of 0.1 The root-mean-square error (RMSE) is the same error that you have seen previously, but having the square-root taken of it. So, to compare with results seen previously, the best error here is as follows:

```
0.08168503^2
```

```
## [1] 0.006672444126
```

A remarkable improvement over a root-mean-square error of 16 we saw earlier.

Neural Networks for Classification

In a sense, we've already demonstrated the use of neural networks for classification via the AND and OR gates that we built at the beginning of the chapter. These functions take some kind of binary input and give us a binary result through logistic regression activation functions at each neural network computational node. You can think of that as single-class classification. Most of the time, we're more interested in multiclass classification.

In this case, you need to split your data into training and test sets, which is straightforward enough. Training the neural network on the training data also makes sense from our past experiences with the train/test approach to machine learning. The difference here is that when you call the predict() function, you do so with the type=class option. This helps when dealing with class data instead of numeric data that you would use with regression:

```
iris.df <- iris
smp_size <- floor(0.75 * nrow(iris.df))

set.seed(123)
train_ind <- sample(seq_len(nrow(iris.df)), size = smp_size)

train <- iris.df[train_ind, ]
test <- iris.df[-train_ind, ]

iris.nnet <- nnet(Species ~ ., data = train, size = 4, decay = 0.0001,
    maxit = 500, trace = FALSE)
predictions <- predict(iris.nnet, test[, 1:4], type = "class")
table(predictions, test$Species)
```

```
##
## predictions  setosa versicolor virginica
##    setosa        11          0         0
##    versicolor     0         13         0
##    virginica      0          0        14
```

You can see that the confusion matrix provides a pretty good result for classification using neural networks. Think back to Chapter 2 and the example that uses kmeans for multiclass clustering; we have no cases here that are mislabeled compared to the two mislabeled cases that we saw previously.

Neural Networks with caret

The machine learning package for R, `caret`, offers a very flexible grouping of tools to use for these machine learning procedures. In the case of neural networks, there are more than 15 to choose from, each with its own advantages and disadvantages. By sticking with our `nnet` example for the moment, we can run a model in `caret` by invoking the `train()` function and passing the `method='nnet'` option to it. We can then go about our normal prediction steps. The power of `caret` comes from the ease with which we can select a different method with which to compare results.

Regression

In the case of regression, the output that you are looking for is going to be numeric. So to compare results across models, you should be looking for an RMSE and then see which one has the lowest, which indicates that this model is the most accurate. For this example, let's use the `Prestige` dataset from the `car` package. This dataset contains a number of features related to occupations and perceived occupational prestige with some features like education, income, and what percentage of incumbents in that profession are women. For this regression example, you'll try to predict income as a function of prestige and education:

```
library(car)
library(caret)
trainIndex <- createDataPartition(Prestige$income, p = 0.7, list = F)
prestige.train <- Prestige[trainIndex, ]
prestige.test <- Prestige[-trainIndex, ]


my.grid <- expand.grid(.decay = c(0.5, 0.1), .size = c(5, 6,
    7))
prestige.fit <- train(income ~ prestige + education, data = prestige.train,
    method = "nnet", maxit = 1000, tuneGrid = my.grid, trace = F,
    linout = 1)

prestige.predict <- predict(prestige.fit, newdata = prestige.test)

summary(prestige.test$income)

##    Min.  1st Qu.   Median     Mean  3rd Qu.     Max.
##  918.000 4230.000 6080.500 7265.214 8088.250 25879.000

sqrt(mean((prestige.predict - prestige.test$income)^2))

## [1] 4118.32384
```

According to the output, the income range in the dataset goes from 611 Canadian dollars up to 17,500. The error being 4,625 Canadian dollars is high, but you can test against other types of neural networks to see how the `nnet` method compares:

```
prestige.fit <- train(income ~ prestige + education, data = prestige.train,
    method = "neuralnet")

prestige.predict <- predict(prestige.fit, newdata = prestige.test)

sqrt(mean((prestige.predict - prestige.test$income)^2))
```

The output from this method is 3,814.09. That's an improvement over the nnet method, but the speed at which this calculation runs is much slower. This is where you need to rely on tuning your training objects to extract the optimal performance out of each different method that you choose.

Classification

Classification with caret works in a similar manner depending on the method you are using. You can use most caret methods for classification or regression, but some are specific to one versus another. The only method that is explicitly classification only for caret is multinom, whereas the methods neuralnet, brnn, qrnn, and mlpSGD are explicitly regression only. You can use the rest for either classification or regression:

```
iris.caret <- train(Species ~ ., data = train, method = "nnet",
    trace = FALSE)
predictions <- predict(iris.caret, test[, 1:4])
table(predictions, test$Species)

##
## predictions  setosa versicolor virginica
##    setosa        11          0         0
##    versicolor     0         13         0
##    virginica      0          0        14
```

The end result here is the same as earlier in terms of model accuracy, but the flexibility of caret allows you again to test against other methods pretty easily:

```
iris.caret.m <- train(Species ~ ., data = train, method = "multinom",
    trace = FALSE)
predictions.m <- predict(iris.caret.m, test[, 1:4])
table(predictions.m, test$Species)

##
## predictions.m setosa versicolor virginica
##    setosa        11          0         0
##    versicolor     0         13         0
##    virginica      0          0        14
```

Good to know that other methods are also quite accurate!

Summary

Neural networks can seem very complicated at first glance. Often they are thought of as a black box; data goes in, and insight comes out. In reality, neural networks are pretty easy to understand in their simplest form, but difficult to explain when they become more complex. At their core, neural networks take some input values, crunch them through an *activation function*, and return an output. The activation function, more often than not, is usually just a sigmoid function, so you can think of neural networks as just more complicated logistic regression models. In fact, their computation with simple neural network architecture is almost identical.

Neural networks become more complex when you begin changing their architecture. A neural network's architecture is made up of an *input layer*, a number of *hidden layers*, and an *output layer*. The input layer is simply the values for what features you are passing in to our model. The hidden layers are those that handle the computation and processing. The output layers are the ones from which you get your results. In simple cases, neural networks can have the hidden computation layers be the same as the output layer, as in the case with modeling logic gate functions like AND and OR. An example neural architecture for a neural network with three inputs, one hidden layer, and one activation node could be 3:1:1, for example. Increasing the number of compute nodes to something like 3:8:1 tends to overfit the data.

Multilayered neural networks (i.e., a 3:2:2:1 neural network) can also model nonlinear behavior. Logistic regression is good at finding decision boundaries that are straight lines to separate data into several classes or types, but it fails for nonlinear behavior. By introducing multiple decision boundaries into a system via hidden layers, you can create a curve that then can separate data, which is something that a straight line cannot do.

You can use neural networks both for regression modeling and classification. However, with regression modeling, it pays to be cautious and practice data normalization. In many cases, neural networks prefer data to be in a 1 or 0 format, and trying to model data that has higher values can be problematic. For classification purposes, when you use the `predict()` function, you also need to pass the `type='class'` option in order to have the modeling behavior work appropriately.

There are a slew of neural network methods that you can use with the `caret` function in R, as well. While some of these are limited to only regression or classification, a good majority of them are flexible enough to be used with either. It pays to be cautious in method selection not just for selecting the one that can do the job you're interested in, but because there can be tuning or optimization parameters that might need to be passed into the model to speed it up or make it more accurate.

## CHAPTER 6

Tree-Based Methods

In the world of machine learning, tree-based methods are very useful. They are relatively simple to explain and easy to visualize. In some cases with machine learning models (notably complex neural networks), the trained model can effectively be a black box whose inner workings are too complex for us to explain simply. Tree-based models, on the other hand, can be a lot more intuitive for the average user.

In this chapter, we look at how tree-based models work at a high level by focusing first on decision trees. We then dive into the basic mechanics of how they work and some positive and negative attributes associated with them. We also touch on different types of tree-based models like conditional inference trees and random forests. To give you a preview, decision trees are as simple as "if-then" statements related to data. Conditional inference trees work in a similar manner but with slightly different statistical underpinnings. Random forests can be complicated mathematically, but generally boil down to a collection of different tree models being asked to vote on a result. All of these types can be used for regression modeling (regression trees) or classification modeling (classification trees). Many can be used for both purposes and are called classification and regression trees (CART) models.

A Simple Tree Model

Let's begin by looking at an example of a set of data that describes my bike races this year. We could have a variety of parameters just related to the weather. If I had a robust enough sample of data and I had a bike race coming up where I knew the forecast to a reasonable degree, should I expect a good or bad result to my bike race? Table 6-1 lists a few different weather factors and what my corresponding race result was.

Table 6-1. Example weather conditions and good race results

Week	Sky condition	Wind speed	Humidity	Good result
1	cloudy	low	high	yes
2	rainy	low	normal	yes
3	sunny	high	normal	yes
4	cloudy	high	high	yes
5	cloudy	low	normal	yes
6	rainy	high	high	no
7	rainy	high	normal	no
8	cloudy	high	normal	yes
9	sunny	low	high	no
10	sunny	low	normal	yes
11	rainy	low	normal	yes
12	sunny	low	high	no
13	sunny	high	high	no

Suppose that the race for week 14 is going to have the following weather:

- Sky Condition: rainy
- Wind speed: low
- Humidity: high

What we might do, if this data were in a spreadsheet, would be to filter our data on those exact conditions and see what the results look like. A tree-based model does basically the same thing. It subsets the data by certain criteria and then builds a tree so that when we have new data, it follows the branches of the tree to a result. Figure 6-1 takes the data from Table 6-1 and represents it as a tree, with the first split being on the Sky Condition variable.

Figure 6-1 shows three leaves in the tree: Sky Condition = rainy, Sky Condition = cloudy, and Sky Condition = sunny. For each of these subsets, you can see how the data looks. The response you want to model is whether I'm going to have a good result in my race. A decision tree looks at these subsets and examines whether the Result variable contains all of one particular class. For cloudy races, I have a good result being yes for each one. This indicates that the subset is pure and that you don't need to split it any further. However, the sunny and rainy subsets have a mix of yes and no results. You'll want to split these further to get a subset with higher purity.

Purity is defined as how many positive or negative examples you have that you're trying to model for (in this case, Result) out of the total values in the table. You want to continue to split the tree until you have as many pure leaves as possible.

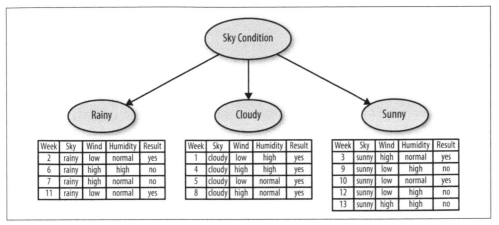

Figure 6-1. An example of how a decision tree subsets data

As Figure 6-2 demonstrates, by splitting up the rainy and sunny subsets further (in this case by wind and humidity, respectively), there are now five terminal points to the tree. You can read this tree like an "if-then" statement, starting at the top. First, let's revisit what you want to predict. You want to know if I'm going to have a good race result if it's rainy, with low wind speed, and high humidity. Begin at the top of the tree and move along the path of Sky Condition = rain, and then split on the wind speed being low. That brings you into a bucket that has all of its data having a good result status of yes. So, based on the conditions that you wanted to predict initially, through the use of a decision tree, you can predict that I'll have a good race result!

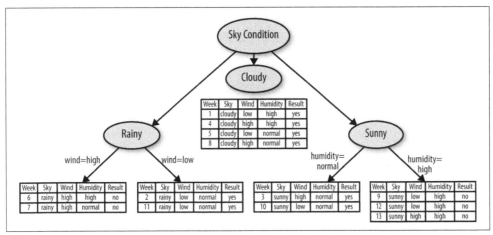

Figure 6-2. This decision tree splits further based on wind speed or humidity to create more resultant tables (or leaves) at the ends of the tree that have a higher purity than before

Deciding How to Split Trees

In the previous example, you started with a dataset that you wanted to model. There were many features and a response against which you wanted to model (result as a function of sky condition, wind speed, and humidity). You began by looking at how a decision tree works by splitting on the variable `Sky Condition`, but why did we choose that one? Why not choose a different variable to split on instead? A decision tree wants to maximize the "purity" of its splits. Let's take a look at Figure 6-3, which revisits the first cut of the tree from earlier.

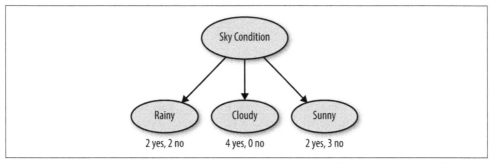

Figure 6-3. When splitting decision trees, you want as pure of leaf nodes as possible (in this case, Cloudy is the most pure leaf, followed by Sunny, then Rainy; we need to split our tree further on the impure leaf nodes to get a better tree model)

In Figure 6-3, the `cloudy` leaf starts out as 100%. That means 100% of the data in that cut is all `yes` data and requires no further subsetting to get to a pure set. The `sunny` and `rainy` leaves do require splitting, however. Let's contrast with starting out with a tree based on the `Wind Speed` variable, as shown in Figure 6-4.

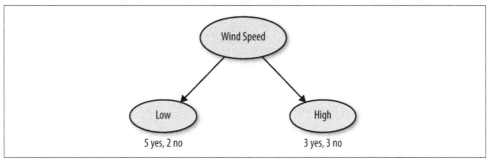

Figure 6-4. Splitting the data based on Wind Speed does not yield results with a high purity factor

In Figure 6-4, none of the initial leaves are totally pure. One leaf is 75% pure, and another is 50%. These both require additional splits of the data. You want to achieve as much purity as you can, and having a tree with one leaf that's 100% pure at the outset points to that variable as the place to start versus the others. Virtually all decision tree algorithms will have this functionality built in, so you don't really ever need to worry about determining an initial split of the data, but it's good practice to know how the underlying mechanics of the tree algorithms work.

Tree Entropy and Information Gain

A more mathematical way to represent the purity of each subset in the tree is to measure its entropy. This is a way to measure how likely you are to get a positive element if you randomly select from a particular subset. The equation for entropy is as follows:

$$H(S) = -p_+ \log_2 p_+ - p_- \log_2 p_-$$

In plain English, this equation states that the entropy for a given set of data is a function of how many positive cases $p+$ we have in total, times the logarithm (note the base two) of the same value, and then subtracting the number of negative cases in the same way. Recall that positive in this case would be a "yes" result, and negative would be a "no" result in the original example data in Table 6-1. A good way to see this in action is to consider how you can apply it to the tree that you split on Sky Condition:

$$H(\text{rainy}) = -\frac{2}{4} log_2 \frac{2}{4} - \frac{2}{4} log_2 \frac{2}{4} = 1$$

$$H(\text{cloudy}) = -\frac{4}{4} log_2 \frac{4}{4} - \frac{0}{4} log_2 \frac{0}{4} = 0$$

$$H(\text{sunny}) = -\frac{2}{5} log_2 \frac{2}{5} - \frac{3}{5} log_2 \frac{3}{5} = 0.97$$

The values you get for rainy and sunny are both 1. This means that the sample is about as impure as you could get and that it would require further splitting, whereas the sample you have for cloudy is totally pure, and the entropy for that is 0. We are getting away with a mathematical trick for this case, because technically speaking the logarithm of zero should be negative infinity, but we are "canceling" that out by multiplying by zero anyway.

Although the entropy of the individual leaves is nice, the algorithm determines the most useful features to split on first by finding the features with the highest *gain*. Gain is a measurement of how relevant the feature is on a scale from 0 (least useful) to 1 (most useful) and is defined by

$$\text{Gain} = H(S) - \Sigma \frac{S_V}{S} H(S_V)$$

where V is the possible values of the feature, S is the number of total points in the leaf, and SV is the subset for which we have our possible values of the feature. Let's run this specifically on the tree that's split by the Wind Speed feature:

$$H(\text{wind}) = -\frac{9}{14} log_2 \frac{9}{14} - \frac{5}{14} log_2 \frac{5}{14} = 0.94$$

$$H(\text{low}) = -\frac{6}{8} log_2 \frac{6}{8} - \frac{2}{8} log_2 \frac{2}{8} = 0.81$$

$$H(\text{high}) = -\frac{3}{6} log_2 \frac{3}{6} - \frac{3}{6} log_2 \frac{3}{6} = 1$$

$$\text{Gain}(\text{Wind}) = 0.94 - \frac{8}{14} * 0.81 - \frac{6}{14} * 1 = 0.049$$

An easy way to do this in R is to use the varImpPlot() function from the caret package. Although this specific function uses a slightly different mathematical computation than Gain specifically, the result is the same. With this plot, you can see that Sky Condition is the most important factor, followed by Humidity and then Wind Speed. If you had a dataset with many more variables and wanted to see which ones a particular tree algorithm thought were the most important, you could use the VarImp Plot() function to get a quick glance to see how to split the tree from the top down:

```
library(caret)
library(randomForest)

cycling <- read.table("cycling.txt", sep = "\t", header = T)

fit <- randomForest(factor(Result) ~ ., data = cycling[2:5])

varImpPlot(fit)
```

Pros and Cons of Decision Trees

So far we've seen one good attribute of decision trees: they are easy to explain. By starting with some sample data, we were able to represent it in a tree-like fashion and then simply walk through the various splits in the data to come to a conclusion. When you train a tree-based model, the underlying mechanics will use the same functionality, so it's very easy to explain how the model itself works.

We've also seen that trees can handle irrelevant data automatically (i.e., when the gain metric is zero). This eliminates the need to be careful in determining which features you want to model against because the tree will almost always select the best attributes for you. Feature selection is a large part of most modeling procedures, and having tree-based models do it for you is a big headache saver.

Another advantage of trees is that they are pretty fast at computation after they've been tuned. In fact, after the tree has been well tuned, the resultant model tends to be quite succinct. This aids not only in explanation, but keeping the model itself relatively simple. It's easy to tell when a tree is overfit when it looks like it's becoming too specific or if there are lots and lots of small branches in the model. Finally, tree-based models can also handle missing or outlier data, again saving you the headache of having to do tedious quarantine procedures that might be more common with other models.

Tree Overfitting

The downsides to trees are that they can be very sensitive to initial conditions or variations in the data. Because we are splitting on attributes and likely value ranges in our data, if we alter values slightly, we could be eliminating entire branches of our model. Another issue with trees is that they follow axis-aligned splits of the data. If we had a tree for some example data, where the output was as follows, we would have a corresponding plot of the data that looks like that shown in Figure 6-5:

- If X is less than 2.5, the result is 25.
- If X is greater than 2.5, and Y is less than 15, the result is 9.
- If X is greater than 2.5, and Y is greater than 15, the result is 3.14.

You can see immediately that trees split the data into boxes, given how they're designed in relation to features. This works better for some versions of data than others. Data that is easily split into boxes relative to the axes that you are splitting by will work better, like in the case of the `iris` dataset illustrated in Figure 6-6.

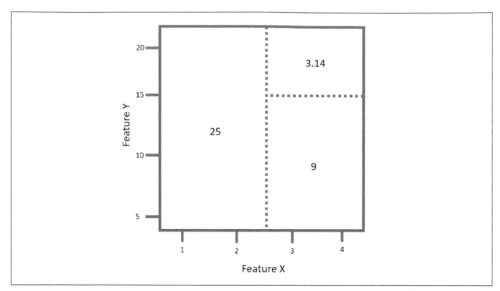

Figure 6-5. Decision trees work in a different fashion than other machine learning algorithms

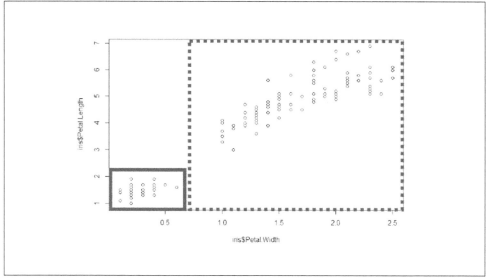

Figure 6-6. Decision trees can classify some data very easily, as seen in the iris dataset

However, data can come in many shapes and sizes. Also from the `iris` dataset is a view of the data that can't be separated by just two or three boxes. Unlike other algorithms that might define a line where all data on one side is class A and all data on the other side is class B, tree-based algorithms must draw boxes to split up data. To approximate a line, or a curve, you need a lot of boxes. What this means for your tree is that you are adding more and more branches and increasing the complexity of it, as depicted in Figure 6-7.

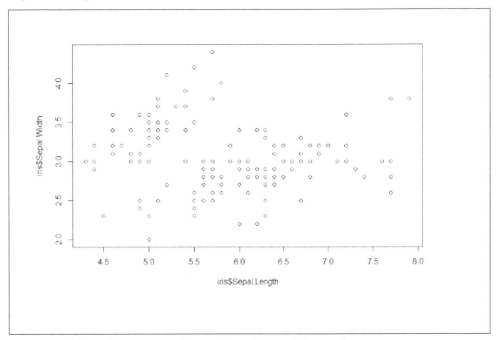

Figure 6-7. Using the same iris dataset, but plotting different data, you come across a situation in which one or two boxes might not fit the data so well

Using many more boxes to split up the data into two halves can likely overfit the data you're trying to use for a regression or classification model, as shown in Figure 6-8.

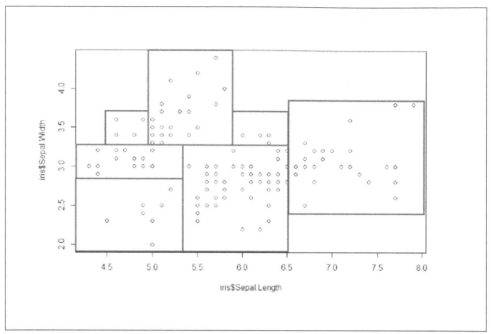

Figure 6-8. Classifying data with a tree-like approach can be susceptible to overfitting, as seen with many small boxes in this plot

As we've seen so far, you build tree-based models by starting with a high gain attribute and then splitting on the next highest gain attributes. In the cycling races example at the beginning of the chapter, there are sufficient examples to build a tree that yielded us pure samples for every leaf at the end of the tree-growing exercise. If you had a dataset that required you to add more and more splits to the tree, the model would become much too specific to the data with which you are training it.

If you take some sample data, split it into a train and test set, and then grow the tree on the training model, you need to find a cut-off point to stop growing the tree. Otherwise, if it grows too much, it won't perform well against test data because the training tree has become too specific to the training data and isn't able to be generalized well, as illustrated in Figure 6-9.

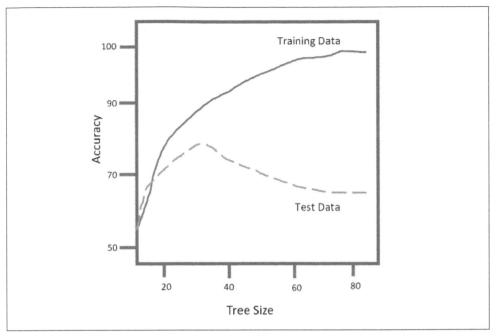

Figure 6-9. Tree-based methods perform well on training data but yield diminishing returns on test data

Pruning Trees

To keep a tree-based model from overfitting, you need to prune the least important leaves of the tree. You can do this through the use of the rpart package. First let's grow a tree by using the rpart() function. This is a function that recursively partitions the data to form a tree-based model. First, let's take a quick look at the data you'll be modeling, which is automobile data from the 1990 edition of Consumer Reports:

```
library(rpart)

head(cu.summary)

##                 Price Country Reliability Mileage  Type
## Acura Integra 4 11950   Japan Much better      NA Small
## Dodge Colt 4     6851   Japan        <NA>      NA Small
## Dodge Omni 4     6995     USA  Much worse      NA Small
## Eagle Summit 4   8895     USA      better      33 Small
## Ford Escort   4  7402     USA       worse      33 Small
## Ford Festiva 4   6319   Korea      better      37 Small
```

For each vehicle in the dataset, there are features related to them that a consumer might be interested in when making an informed purchase. Features include Price, which is the cost of the car in US dollars; `Country` of origin; `Reliability` scaling from "much worse" to "average" to "much better"; `Mileage` in units of gallons of fuel consumed per mile; and what `Type` the car is (compact, large, medium, small, sporty, van).

Let's grow a tree based on this data using the `rpart()` function (Figure 6-10):

```
fit <- rpart(
  Mileage~Price + Country + Reliability + Type,
    method="anova", #method="class" for classificaiton tree
  data=cu.summary
  )

plot(fit, uniform=TRUE, margin=0.1)
text(fit, use.n=TRUE, all=TRUE, cex=.8)
```

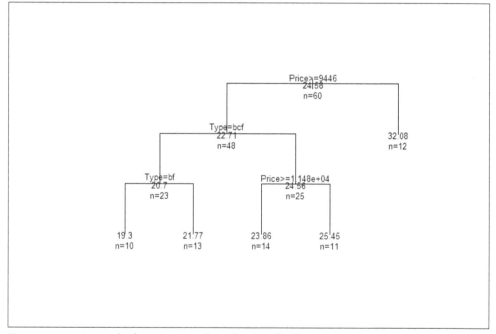

Figure 6-10. A simple decision tree plotted using the rpart() function from the rpart library; here, we start with feature Price and split accordingly

Specific to the `rpart()` function, the `method=` option allows you to switch between using a regression tree and a classification tree. In this case, you're modeling a vehicle's fuel efficiency, as given by the `Mileage` variable, which is a numeric value, so you want a regression model as a result. You can see the result of this in Figure 6-10. Reading from top to bottom, you first split on `Price` being greater than or equal to $9,446. Then, you split on `Type`. Next, for the leftmost branch, split on `Type` again, and for the rightmost branch at the bottom, split on `Price` again. `rpart` indicates what percentage of each branch is split and how many data points are in each split, as well.

Figure 6-11 presents this tree's error rate as a function of how many splits it has:

```
rsq.rpart(fit)[1]
```

```
##
## Regression tree:
## rpart(formula = Mileage ~ Price + Country + Reliability + Type,
##     data = cu.summary, method = "anova")
##
## Variables actually used in tree construction:
## [1] Price Type
##
## Root node error: 1354.6/60 = 22.576
##
## n=60 (57 observations deleted due to missingness)
##
##         CP nsplit rel error  xerror     xstd
## 1 0.622885      0   1.00000 1.02714 0.177370
## 2 0.132061      1   0.37711 0.52743 0.100904
## 3 0.025441      2   0.24505 0.39710 0.081674
## 4 0.011604      3   0.21961 0.37697 0.081364
## 5 0.010000      4   0.20801 0.39218 0.079890
```

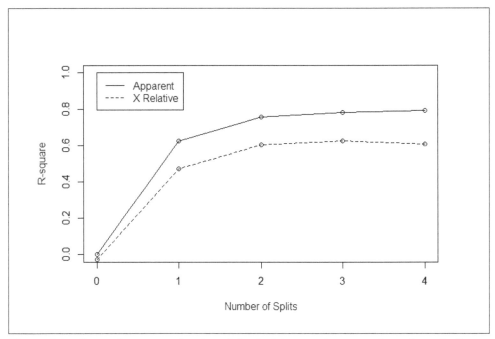

Figure 6-11. Error plots versus the size of the decision tree in terms of number of splits

Using the `rsq.rpart()` function gives us two plots. Figure 6-12 shows the accuracy of the tree-based model compared with the number of splits in the tree. Figure 6-12 shows us the relative error also as a function of the number of splits in the tree. It seems pretty clear from these two plots that the tree is pretty well tuned at splits 2 and 3, and that adding another split to get a total of 4 doesn't seem to add much value to the model.

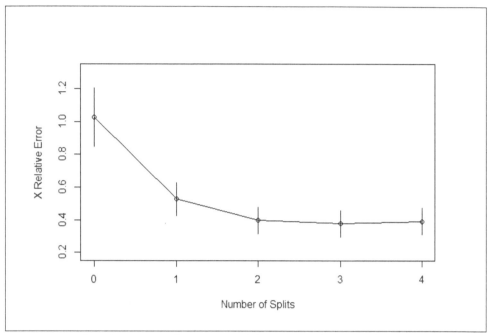

Figure 6-12. The relative error from cross-validation as a function of the number of splits

To clean up the model and ensure that it isn't being overfit, prune the less useful leaves of the tree. A more precise way of knowing which parts to prune is to look at a tree's *complexity parameter*, often referred to as the "CP," which you can see in Figure 6-13:

```
plotcp(fit)
```

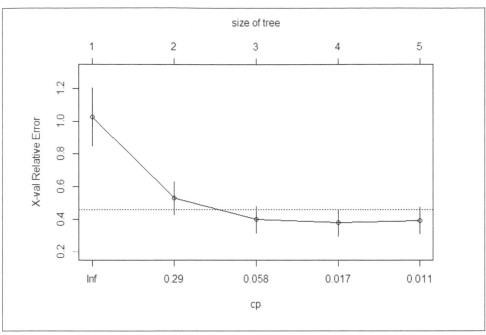

Figure 6-13. You can add a dotted-line threshold that signifies the best cp value to choose —in this case, 0.058 and a tree size of 3

The complexity parameter is the amount by which splitting that tree node will improve the relative error. In Figure 6-13, splitting it once improved the error by 0.29, and then less so for each additional split. The dotted line on the plot is generated by error estimations within the model and signals that you want a tree that has a number of splits below that line, but maybe not too far beyond it to avoid overfitting. The y-axis is the relative error for a given node, as well. You can see from the plot that the relative error is minimized at a tree size of 4 (upper x-axis) and the complexity parameter is below the dotted line threshold. Note that the tree size is the number of splits in the data, not the number of terminal leaves. The general rule to follow is to select the first complexity parameter that is beneath the dotted line. In this case, though, you can see that there are minor gains in error evaluation to be had at the next step in the tree size at 4, or complexity parameter equal to 0.017.

You can extract these values programmatically from the model's `cptable`, as follows:

```
fit$cptable
```

```
##            CP nsplit rel error    xerror       xstd
## 1 0.62288527      0 1.0000000 1.0271438 0.17736964
## 2 0.13206061      1 0.3771147 0.5274319 0.10090361
## 3 0.02544094      2 0.2450541 0.3970990 0.08167442
```

```
## 4 0.01160389      3 0.2196132 0.3769729 0.08136370
## 5 0.01000000      4 0.2080093 0.3921772 0.07988950
```

You can see that the error is minimized at tree size of 4. Thus, let's use the xerror value at 4 in the prune() function (Figure 6-14) to cut off any splits beyond that level of complexity:

```
fit.pruned <- prune(fit, cp = fit$cptable[which.min(fit$cptable[,
    "xerror"]), "CP"])

par(mfrow = c(1, 2))

plot(fit, uniform = TRUE, margin = 0.1, main = "Original Tree")
text(fit, use.n = TRUE, all = TRUE, cex = 0.8)

plot(fit.pruned, uniform = TRUE, margin = 0.1, main = "Pruned Tree")
text(fit.pruned, use.n = TRUE, all = TRUE, cex = 0.8)
```

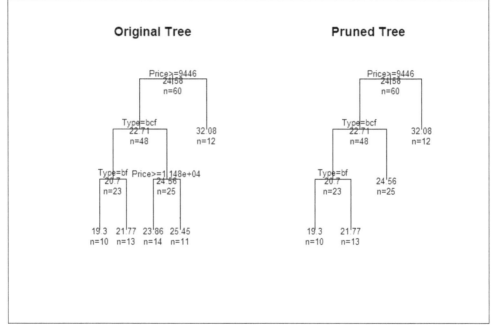

Figure 6-14. A pruned tree; compared to Figure 6-10, we have lopped off one branch entirely and saved some error involved with the model as a result

This example takes the complexity parameter, cp, and passes it to the prune() function to effectively eliminate any splits that don't make the model reduce its error.

Decision Trees for Regression

We've covered a lot of ground in this section with respect to decision trees and how to tune them for best performance. If you want to do a simple regression model using rpart() functionality with decision trees, you first need to grow the tree and then prune it, as demonstrated here:

```
cu.summary.complete <- cu.summary[complete.cases(cu.summary),]
data.samples <- sample(1:nrow(cu.summary.complete), nrow(cu.summary.complete) *
0.7, replace = FALSE)
training.data <- cu.summary.complete[data.samples, ]
test.data <- cu.summary.complete[-data.samples, ]

fit <- rpart(
  Mileage~Price + Country + Reliability + Type,
   method="anova", #method="class" for classification tree
  data=training.data
  )

fit.pruned<- prune(fit, cp=fit$cptable[which.min(fit$cptable[,"xerror"]),"CP"])

prediction <- predict(fit.pruned, test.data)

output <- data.frame(test.data$Mileage, prediction)

RMSE = sqrt(sum((output$test.data.Mileage - output$prediction)^2) /
      nrow(output))
RMSE

## [1] 2.318792
```

Decision Trees for Classification

Repeating the exercise with rpart() for classification is trivial. All you need to do is switch the method option from anova to class, as well as switch the response that you're modeling to an actual class variable:

```
cu.summary.complete <- cu.summary[complete.cases(cu.summary),
    ]
data.samples <- sample(1:nrow(cu.summary.complete), nrow(cu.summary.complete) *
    0.7, replace = FALSE)
training.data <- cu.summary.complete[data.samples, ]
test.data <- cu.summary.complete[-data.samples, ]

fit <- rpart(Type ~ Price + Country + Reliability + Mileage,
    method = "class", data = training.data)

fit.pruned <- prune(fit, cp = fit$cptable[which.min(fit$cptable[,
    "xerror"]), "CP"])

prediction <- predict(fit.pruned, test.data, type = "class")
```

```
table(prediction, test.data$Type)

##
## prediction Compact Large Medium Small Sporty Van
##    Compact       2     0      1     1      2   0
##    Large         0     0      0     0      0   0
##    Medium        1     1      2     0      1   0
##    Small         0     0      0     4      0   0
##    Sporty        0     0      0     0      0   0
##    Van           0     0      0     0      0   0
```

Conditional Inference Trees

A slightly different type of decision tree is a *conditional inference tree*. Previously, we saw how to grow and prune a decision tree as built from the `rpart()` function in R. That function builds a tree by selecting features with high values related to information gain. In many cases, we need to prune those types of trees to keep them from being overfit and having a bit too much error per tree split.

In contrast, a conditional inference tree follows very similar logic, but the way we split the tree is slightly different. A conditional inference tree will lean more heavily on robust statistical tests for a given feature to determine its statistical significance.

We can see this illustrated by plotting a conditional inference tree from a model fit using the `ctree()` function from the happily named `party` package, as depicted in Figure 6-15:

```
library(party)

fit2 <- ctree(Mileage ~ Price + Country + Reliability + Type,
    data = na.omit(cu.summary))

plot(fit2)
```

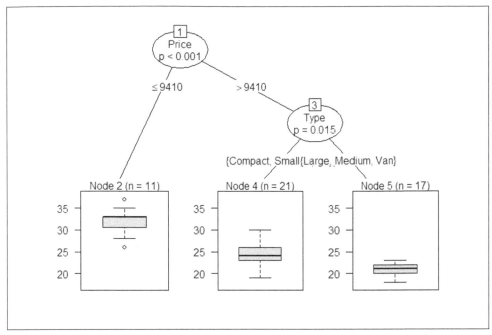

Figure 6-15. A decision tree plotted using the ctree() function from the party library

Like many R packages, some are better for plotting than others. Although there are options to make trees made from `rpart()` plots prettier, `ctree()` makes better looking visuals out of the box. In Figure 6-15, you can see a tree comprising two features, `Price` and `Type`, that are being split. The splitting criteria can be found on the branches like always, but there's a new parameter: the *p*-value. These are the values inside the bubbles that show the feature on which we're splitting. A *p*-value is a tool for measuring how statistically significant something is. The rule that statisticians follow is that a *p*-value below 0.05 is considered statistically significant. No pruning for this particular type of tree is necessary, because that is built in to the statistical procedures that select the features to split on in the first place, saving you a step of calculation down the line.

Likewise, if you want to plot the tree for a classification scheme, instead, all you would need to do is provide a factor variable response and repeat the same plotting procedure, as demonstrated in Figure 6-16:

```
fit3 <- ctree(Type ~ Price + Country + Reliability + Mileage,
    data = na.omit(cu.summary))

plot(fit3)
```

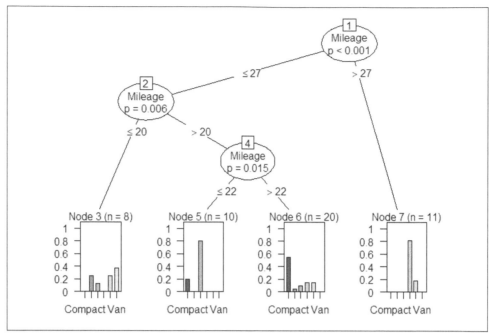

Figure 6-16. A classification model from the ctree() function plotted can sometimes have outputs that are difficult to view when there are many classes involved

If you have many factor variables, plotting the tree can be a little cumbersome because the plot by default includes values that are zero for a given split of the data.

Conditional Inference Tree Regression

Running a regression model using conditional inference trees will look familiar. Given that almost all machine learning models in R follow the same basic pattern of "function(response ~ features)," it should come as no surprise that performing regression using `ctree` will follow the same formula:

```
set.seed(123)

cu.summary.complete <- cu.summary[complete.cases(cu.summary),
    ]
data.samples <- sample(1:nrow(cu.summary.complete), nrow(cu.summary.complete) *
    0.7, replace = FALSE)
training.data <- cu.summary.complete[data.samples, ]
test.data <- cu.summary.complete[-data.samples, ]

fit.ctree <- ctree(Mileage ~ Price + Country + Reliability +
    Type, data = training.data)

prediction.ctree <- predict(fit.ctree, test.data)
```

```
output <- data.frame(test.data$Mileage, prediction.ctree)

RMSE = sqrt(sum((output$test.data.Mileage - output$Mileage)^2)/nrow(output))
RMSE

## [1] 3.37476
```

Conditional Inference Tree Classification

Performing a classification model in R is just as easy. Because you've already done the process with a regression example, all you need to do for a classification example is change the response you're using from a numeric to a categorical one:

```
set.seed(456)

data.samples <- sample(1:nrow(cu.summary), nrow(cu.summary) *
    0.7, replace = FALSE)
training.data <- cu.summary[data.samples, ]
test.data <- cu.summary[-data.samples, ]

fit.ctree <- ctree(Type ~ Price + Country + Reliability + Mileage,
    data = training.data)

prediction.ctree <- predict(fit.ctree, test.data)

table(test.data$Type, prediction.ctree)

##           prediction.ctree
##            Compact Large Medium Small Sporty Van
##  Compact        2     0      5     1      0   0
##  Large          1     0      1     0      0   1
##  Medium         2     0      5     0      0   0
##  Small          2     0      0     4      0   0
##  Sporty         7     0      0     2      0   1
##  Van            1     0      0     0      0   1
```

Random Forests

The tree-based methods we've dealt with so far have all been a single tree. That is, the "if-then" logic of starting with a feature, splitting based on value ranges in that feature, and then moving down the tree to a final result is how a single decision tree works. One of the most cutting-edge forms of machine learning is a *random forest*. Instead of growing one single tree, we're going to grow *N* different trees. We get different trees by randomizing our inputs to the algorithm that builds the trees for us.

Each tree will have some kind of output based on the feature splits in the data, like we've seen for tree-based models thus far. The difference is that we take the results from each tree and tally which output has the most votes. The output with the most votes becomes the output for the forest.

In an example of classification, we might have a group of trees that look like that shown in Figure 6-17.

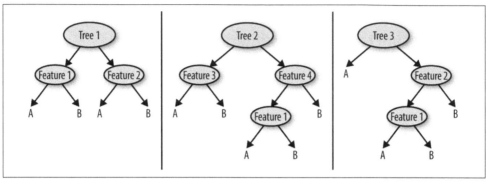

Figure 6-17. An example of how a random forest model works

We have three trees, each with a class A or B output. Notice that the trees have different features on which they might be splitting, as well. Because you are building the trees from random subsets of your starting data, various subsets might have different splitting parameters than other subsets.

The next step would be to pass some kind of input into the forest of three trees. Suppose that after you pass the input into each tree, you get a prediction like this:

- Tree 1: A
- Tree 2: B
- Tree 3: A

You then take a majority vote of the classes that are output from the trees to get the final answer from the random forest. In this case, the answer for the forest would be class A.

Random Forest Regression

Regression with random forests in R is as easy as replacing what feature you're modeling on as the response. All you need to do in this case to change from a conditional inference tree to a random forest is change the function call that you're using on the training data, as demonstrated here:

```
library(randomForest)
set.seed(123)

cu.summary.complete <- cu.summary[complete.cases(cu.summary),
```

```
    ]
data.samples <- sample(1:nrow(cu.summary.complete), nrow(cu.summary.complete) *
    0.7, replace = FALSE)
training.data <- cu.summary.complete[data.samples, ]
test.data <- cu.summary.complete[-data.samples, ]

fit.rf <- randomForest(Mileage ~ Price + Country + Reliability +
    Type, data = training.data)

prediction.rf <- predict(fit.rf, test.data)

output <- data.frame(test.data$Mileage, prediction.rf)

RMSE = sqrt(sum((output$test.data.Mileage - output$prediction.rf)^2)/
      nrow(output))
RMSE

## [1] 3.260948
```

Random Forest Classification

Likewise, setting up code in R for classification with random forests is as easy as before, but you just set the function specifically to randomForest():

```
set.seed(456)

cu.summary.complete <- cu.summary[complete.cases(cu.summary),
    ]
data.samples <- sample(1:nrow(cu.summary.complete), nrow(cu.summary.complete) *
    0.7, replace = FALSE)
training.data <- cu.summary.complete[data.samples, ]
test.data <- cu.summary.complete[-data.samples, ]

fit.rf <- randomForest(Type ~ Price + Country + Reliability +
    Mileage, data = training.data)

prediction.rf <- predict(fit.rf, test.data)

table(test.data$Type, prediction.rf)

##          prediction.rf
##          Compact Large Medium Small Sporty Van
## Compact       3     0      1     0      0   0
## Large         0     0      1     0      0   0
## Medium        0     0      1     0      0   0
## Small         0     0      0     4      0   0
## Sporty        1     0      0     0      2   0
## Van           0     0      0     0      1   1
```

Summary

In this chapter, we discussed machine learning models in R related to tree-based methods. A tree can be as simple as a pictographic representation of "if-then" statements but modeled in a top-down fashion where you move along branches of the tree depending on the outcome of those statements.

Tree-based models in general are useful because of their ability to handle missing data and outliers, and they're reasonably compact. Their primary strength lies in simplicity, though. It's a lot easier to draw a decision tree on a whiteboard than it would be for many other machine learning algorithms.

Decision tree algorithms work by ranking the features in a dataset by a specific parameter, sometimes by information gain, other times by statistical measurements like p-values. You start a tree with the most important variable, then split it based on conditions, and repeat as necessary. In some cases you might need to prune your trees to keep them from having too many branches and becoming overfit to the data with which you are training them.

Finally, we touched on random forest machine learning. A random forest is a collection of different decision trees generated from random starting data, which is taken as random subsets from your training set. These trees will then each take input data and give a guess as to what they think the answer is. When all the trees in the forest have an answer, a final answer is determined by majority vote.

## CHAPTER 7

Other Advanced Methods

In this chapter, we show off a miscellany of machine learning models available in R. Even though the main algorithms that we've covered thus far really make up the majority of models, I wanted to include this chapter to provide a comprehensive view of the machine learning ecosystem in R.

We cover classification again, but through the lens of Bayesian statistics. This is a popular field of statistics and helps to transition to some other algorithms that depend on similar logic. We also cover principal component analysis, support vector machines, and *k*-nearest neighbor algorithms.

Naive Bayes Classification

One way to do classification with probabilities is through the use of *Bayesian statistics*. Although this field can have a rather steep learning curve, essentially we are trying to answer the question, "Based on the features we have, what is the probability that the outcome is class *X*?" A naive Bayes classifier answers this question with a rather bold assumption: all of the predictors we have are independent of one another. The advantage to doing this is that we drastically reduce the complexity of the calculations we're doing.

Bayesian Statistics in a Nutshell

Bayesian statistics relies a lot on multiplication of probabilities. Let's do a quick primer on this so you're up to speed. Suppose that I ride my bike in 100 races and I win 54 of them (if only!). The probability of me winning a race, therefore, is just the number of times I've won divided by the total number of occurrences:

$P(\text{win}) = 54/100 = 54\,\%$

Now let's talk about independent and dependent probabilities. Suppose that I want to learn the probability of me winning a bike race *and* the probability of a wind storm occurring on Mars. These two things are completely independent of each other, given that there being a wind storm on Mars could not possibly affect the result of my bike race, and vice versa. Let's assume that the probability of a wind storm on Mars is 20%. To calculate the probability of both of these independent things happening, we just multiply them:

$$P(\text{win and Mars}) = P(\text{win}) \times P(\text{Mars}) = 54\% \times 20\% = 10.8\%$$

However, if two events are dependent, we need to use a slightly different approach. Consider a deck of cards. The probability of me picking any queen is 4/52. The probability of me picking any ace after picking out a queen, however, is dependent, because we just removed a card from the deck; thus, probability would now be 4/51. The probability would be defined like this:

$$P(\text{Queen and Ace}) = P(\text{Queen}) \times P(\text{Ace} \mid \text{Queen}) = (4/52) \times (4/51) = 0.6\%$$

We can rewrite our probability like this:

$$P(A \text{ and } B) = P(A) * P(B \mid A)$$

and rearrange to give it another form:

$$P(A \text{ and } B) = P(A) * P(B \mid A)$$

$$\frac{P(A \text{ and } B)}{P(A)} = P(B \mid A)$$

$$\frac{P(B) * P(A \mid B)}{P(A)} = P(B \mid A)$$

In plain English, this is what these steps say:

1. Start with the probability of A and B, which is the probability of A multiplied by the probability of B, given A.
2. Divide the probability of A and B by just the probability of A.
3. Replace the probability of A and B on the left side with the starting definition.

What we have as a result is the naive Bayes formula. This tells us the conditional probabilities of an event given prior information or evidence about the features that we're looking at. The "naive" part comes from the bold assertion that the features we are interested in are independent.

Application of Naive Bayes

Let's apply this mathematical formulation in R. The library `e1071` has a useful function, `naiveBayes()`, for building models of this type. By using the aforementioned Bayes rule, you can calculate conditional probabilities of a categorical class. In this case, let's use data related to breast cancer studies done by the University of Wisconsin Hospitals and Clinics. There are nine features in this dataset, with one column being an ID value that is of no interest, and one other column being the `Class` designation for the type of cell, where 2 represents a benign cell and 4 represents a malignant cell. The rest of the features pertain to the cell being studied, with features like "Uniformity of Cell Size" and "Single Epithelial Cell Size." Here's the code:

```
# https://archive.ics.uci.edu/ml/machine-learning-databases/breast-cancer-
wisconsin/

library(e1071)

breast_cancer <- data.frame(read.table("breast_cancer.txt", header = T,
    sep = "\t"))

names(breast_cancer) <- c("SampleCodeNumber", "ClumpThickness",
    "UniformityofCellSize", "UniformityofCellShape", "MarginalAdhesion",
    "SingleEpithelialCellSize", "BareNuclei", "BlandChromatin",
    "NormalNucleoli", "Mitoses", "Class")

breast_cancer <- data.frame(sapply(breast_cancer, as.factor))

breast_cancer_features <- breast_cancer[, 2:11]

nb.model <- naiveBayes(Class ~ ., data = breast_cancer_features)

print(nb.model)
```

```
Naive Bayes Classifier for Discrete Predictors

Call:
naiveBayes.default(x = x, y = y, laplace = laplace)

A-priori probabilities:
Y
        2         4
0.6359833 0.3640167

Conditional probabilities:
   ClumpThickness
Y            1         10          2          3          4          5          6          7          8          9
  2 0.29934211 0.00000000 0.09539474 0.21710526 0.16118421 0.18750000 0.02631579 0.00000000 0.01315789 0.00000000
  4 0.01724138 0.28160920 0.02298851 0.04597701 0.05172414 0.19540230 0.09195402 0.09770115 0.12643678 0.06896552

   UniformityofCellSize
Y            1         10          2          3          4          5          6          7          8          9
  2 0.845394737 0.000000000 0.088815789 0.036184211 0.019736842 0.000000000 0.000000000 0.003289474 0.003289474 0.003289474
  4 0.022988506 0.298850575 0.028735632 0.103448276 0.126436782 0.120689655 0.097701149 0.068965517 0.109195402 0.022988506

   UniformityofCellShape
Y            1         10          2          3          4          5          6          7          8          9
  2 0.782894737 0.000000000 0.118421053 0.053921053 0.029605263 0.000000000 0.003289474 0.006578947 0.003289474 0.000000000
  4 0.011494253 0.275862069 0.028735632 0.103448276 0.132183908 0.109195402 0.091954023 0.103448276 0.120689655 0.022988506
```

What you see as an output from the model are a couple of different properties. First, there are the "a-priori probabilities," which inform you about the class distribution for the dependent variable that you're modeling.

The second property is the "conditional probabilities." This is a list of tables, one for each predictor variable. Note in the image that I've truncated the output so that it doesn't totally dominate the page with output from all the different features. However, for each of the features, there are condition probabilities for the factors of the response. So, for example, the ClumpThickness feature has 10 different categorical variables in it. For each one of those categories, there are the conditional probabilities of cell class. Recall that class 2 means the cell is benign, whereas class 4 indicates that it's malignant. This tabular output lets you see in fine granular detail the naive Bayes probabilities for each of the features.

The next logical step is to utilize this algorithm for predictive purposes. You can do this by following the same tried-and-true method of splitting the data into training and test sets, modeling on the training set, and then outputting a confusion matrix of the predictor variable:

```
breast_cancer_complete <-
    breast_cancer_features[complete.cases(breast_cancer_features),
    ]
breast_cancer_complete$Class <- as.factor(breast_cancer_complete$Class)
data.samples <- sample(1:nrow(breast_cancer_complete),
    nrow(breast_cancer_complete) *
    0.7, replace = FALSE)

training.data <- breast_cancer_complete[data.samples, ]
test.data <- breast_cancer_complete[-data.samples, ]

nb.model <- naiveBayes(Class ~ ., data = training.data)

prediction.nb <- predict(nb.model, test.data)

table(test.data$Class, prediction.nb)

##      prediction.nb
##        2    4
##    2 129    4
##    4   0   72
```

Here, we see that the naive Bayes model seems to work pretty well, giving us a fairly accurately predicted output.

Principal Component Analysis

Principal component analysis (PCA) is a kind of machine learning that we use as a data preprocessing step to help with a few different approaches. In many cases of data analysis, we might have features that are highly correlated with one another. If we were to blast that data with a machine learning model without any kind of feature selection beforehand, we might get some extra error in our modeling procedure because some of our features could be highly correlated.

For example, if you want to model sales of a product as a function of econometrics of various countries, you might have some data that could have features like Country, Year, Population, Percent of Broadband Users, Percent of Urban Population, GDP, GDP Per capita, Poverty Index, Life Expectancy, and so forth. In theory, some of these values are very dependent on one another, like GDP and Population. In some cases, they might be linearly correlated. The function of PCA in this case would be to reduce that correlation between GDP and Population to just one feature, which would be the functional relation between the two.

If you had some kind of example dataset with 30 or 40 features, but most of them were highly correlated with one another, you could run a PCA algorithm on it and reduce the data to just two features. This would reduce the computational complexity of the dataset considerably.

Using PCA, you could reduce your data from something that looks like this

```
head(mtcars)
```

```
##                      mpg cyl disp  hp drat    wt  qsec vs am gear carb
## Mazda RX4           21.0   6  160 110 3.90 2.620 16.46  0  1    4    4
## Mazda RX4 Wag       21.0   6  160 110 3.90 2.875 17.02  0  1    4    4
## Datsun 710          22.8   4  108  93 3.85 2.320 18.61  1  1    4    1
## Hornet 4 Drive      21.4   6  258 110 3.08 3.215 19.44  1  0    3    1
## Hornet Sportabout   18.7   8  360 175 3.15 3.440 17.02  0  0    3    2
## Valiant             18.1   6  225 105 2.76 3.460 20.22  1  0    3    1
```

to a more compact form, like this:

```
##                          x1       x2
## Mazda RX4         1.5560338 2.391719
## Mazda RX4 Wag     1.1481763 2.754611
## Datsun 710        0.2824424 2.622031
## Hornet 4 Drive    3.7019535 2.806743
## Hornet Sportabout 3.2649748 2.483172
## Valiant           4.1630202 2.048424
```

PCA's usefulness for dimensionality reduction of data can be helpful for visualizing complex data patterns. Human brains are very adept at visualization and we can read a two-dimensional chart very well. Three-dimensional visualizations can be easily discerned by the brain in real life but are a bit trickier to see on a computer screen, which itself is a two-dimensional plane. PCA can help us take complex data and visualize it in a more compact space for easier analysis. Figure 7-1 shows an example of data that could use a PCA pass:

```
pairs(mtcars[, 1:7], lower.panel = NULL)
```

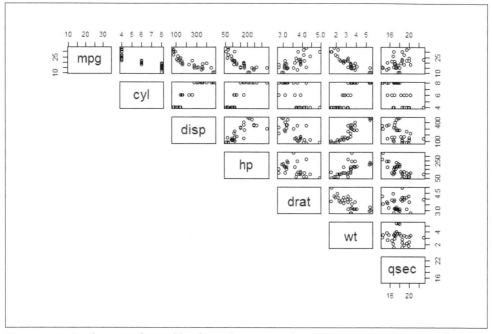

Figure 7-1. A selection of variables from the mtcars dataset; you can use PCA to find correlations in the data and reduce the complexity of the dataset for future processing

In the mtcars dataset, there is a good number of features, some of which look like they might be correlated with one another. A good general practice before applying PCA is to take a glance at your data and see whether there are indeed any values that look like they might be correlated.

At first glance of the data, it looks like there are some well-correlated values, with many of them corresponding to the vehicle's weight variable, wt. Let's walk through how you can reduce some of these variables' dependencies and generate a more simplified picture of the data.

In R, there are two functions that are pretty similar in terms of syntax that can do PCA out of the box: princomp and prcomp. One of your first objectives is to visualize how much of the variance a certain number of principal components can explain in your data. The princomp function has some simple built-in functionality that lends itself better for plotting, so let's use princomp for the moment:

```
pca <- princomp(mtcars, scores = TRUE, cor = TRUE)
```

You can use the argument score to store some data used for scoring each component, which we'll come to in a second. The cor argument aligns with using a correlation matrix for calculations instead of a covariance matrix. The differences are subtle and kind of dependent on the data or the type of calculation that you want to do, but we'll be getting too deep into the statistical weeds going down that road, so just use the correlation matrix for now.

Let's take a look at the output from the pca object:

```
summary(pca)

## Importance of components:
##                           Comp.1     Comp.2     Comp.3     Comp.4
## Standard deviation     2.5706809 1.6280258 0.79195787 0.51922773
## Proportion of Variance 0.6007637 0.2409516 0.05701793 0.02450886
## Cumulative Proportion  0.6007637 0.8417153 0.89873322 0.92324208
##                           Comp.5     Comp.6     Comp.7     Comp.8
## Standard deviation     0.47270615 0.45999578 0.36777981 0.35057301
## Proportion of Variance 0.02031374 0.01923601 0.01229654 0.01117286
## Cumulative Proportion  0.94355581 0.96279183 0.97508837 0.98626123
##                            Comp.9    Comp.10     Comp.11
## Standard deviation     0.277572792 0.228112781 0.148473587
## Proportion of Variance 0.007004241 0.004730495 0.002004037
## Cumulative Proportion  0.993265468 0.997995963 1.000000000
```

This table shows how important each of these mysterious principal components are to the overall dataset. The row that you're most interested in is the Proportion of Variance, which tells you how much of the data is explained by that principal component. The components are always sorted by how important they are, so the most important components will always be the first few. In the preceding output, you can see that component 1 explains 60% of the data, with component 2 coming in at 24%, and then a steep drop-off for the rest. If you want to represent this data graphically, follow the example shown in Figure 7-2:

```
plot(pca)
```

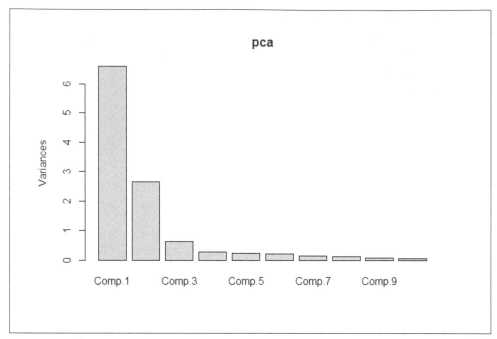

Figure 7-2. The variances of our various components; this is a more visual way to see how much our main components explain the data

This plot of component importance indicates that the main first component explains a large chunk of the data. Combined with component 2, this explains upward of 84% of the dataset with just two features instead of the 11 that we started with.

But these principal components sound kind of mysterious. What does component 1 mean to us as humans or decision makers? In PCA, you can look at the loadings to see how much of each variable is contained in each component that you're looking at:

```
pca$loadings[, 1:5]
```

```
##             Comp.1      Comp.2      Comp.3       Comp.4      Comp.5
## mpg     0.3625305 -0.01612440 -0.22574419 -0.022540255 -0.10284468
## cyl    -0.3739160 -0.04374371 -0.17531118 -0.002591838 -0.05848381
## disp   -0.3681852  0.04932413 -0.06148414  0.256607885 -0.39399530
## hp     -0.3300569 -0.24878402  0.14001476 -0.067676157 -0.54004744
## drat    0.2941514 -0.27469408  0.16118879  0.854828743 -0.07732727
## wt     -0.3461033  0.14303825  0.34181851  0.245899314  0.07502912
## qsec    0.2004563  0.46337482  0.40316904  0.068076532  0.16466591
## vs      0.3065113  0.23164699  0.42881517 -0.214848616 -0.59953955
## am      0.2349429 -0.42941765 -0.20576657 -0.030462908 -0.08978128
## gear    0.2069162 -0.46234863  0.28977993 -0.264690521 -0.04832960
## carb   -0.2140177 -0.41357106  0.52854459 -0.126789179  0.36131875
```

These values are the correlations between the principal component and the features with which you started. This example shows just the first five principal components to save space, as components 6 through 9 are not really that useful anyway.

The closer the correlation number is to 1 or –1 for each combination of component and feature, the more that feature is important to that component. Let's look at component 1. This one has a balance of all the starting features, with mpg being the dominant positive value, and cyl being the dominant negative value. Component 2 is mostly dominated by the variables qsec, gear, and am, in that order. Likewise for the rest of the components.

So, if you had to ascribe some sort of relation between the components and the features, you would say that:

- Component 1 is correlated to mpg and cyl
- Component 2 is correlated to qsec, gear, and am

If you wanted to see this kind of information in a more graphical sense, you can plot the scores of the principal components, as shown in Figure 7-3:

```
scores.df <- data.frame(pca$scores)
scores.df$car <- row.names(scores.df)

plot(x = scores.df$Comp.1, y = scores.df$Comp.2, xlab = "Comp1 (mpg,cyl)",
    ylab = "Comp2 (qsec, gear, am)")

text(scores.df$Comp.1, scores.df$Comp.2, labels = scores.df$car,
    cex = 0.7, pos = 3)
```

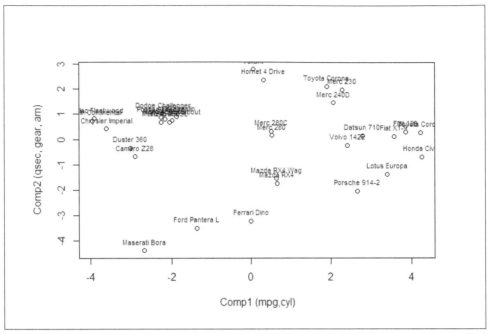

Figure 7-3. A plot of the data as a function of the two principal components; cars on this plot that are grouped together are very similar to one another based on the components used to describe them

What we've done as this last stage is to show that a lot of the data can be compressed into two principal components: one having to do mostly with the `mpg` and `cyl` variables, and the other being a combination of `qsec`, `gear`, and `am` variables. In Figure 7-3, you can see that some cars fall into certain ends of the spectrum versus others and might be very well related to one another based on many factors that are compressed into just one or two variables.

Notice that the values of the axes here are also somewhat different than the starting variable values. This is because some PCA algorithms have built-in feature scaling techniques that make sure all of the variables are within the same range of one another for comparison's sake; otherwise, if you had one variable (like the vehicle's weight) that could be hundreds or thousands of times bigger than another variable (like number of cylinders), the analysis could be very misleading. With the `princomp` function, this feature scaling is built in, but other PCA algorithms in R might require you to explicitly enable scaling.

Linear Discriminant Analysis

PCA seeks to find a series of vectors that describe variance in the data. For example, you might have some data described by two features, X and Y, that you can plot. You can find a couple vectors that explain how much the data varies in one direction versus an orthogonal direction to the first vector, as depicted in Figure 7-4.

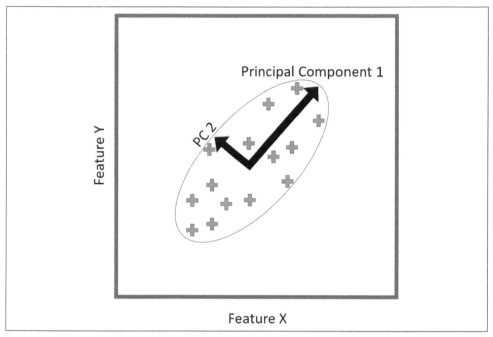

Figure 7-4. Principal components describe the variance in the data; here, there are two component vectors, with the principal component being the one describing the longer of the two axes in the data

More complex datasets might have more features and more vectors, but the idea is the same. In contrast, a different way to do feature analysis would be with linear discriminant analysis (LDA). In this case, you might have some data that is a function of X and Y, again, but this time, as Figure 7-5 shows, you want to classify them into different groups based on how their data are distributed.

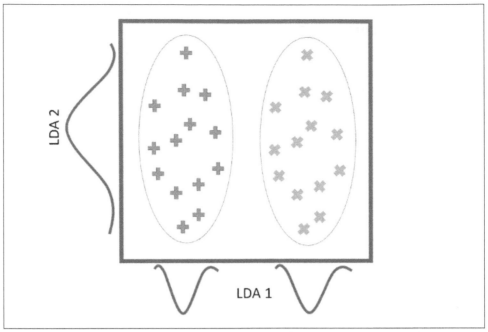

Figure 7-5. LDA describes how best to separate data based on classes; here, there is a set of data that's effectively split by the distributions along the X-axis and Y-axis, respectively

In Figure 7-5, there is some data that's plotted, but separated into two classes. The + data has a distribution across the X-axis, as does the other data. The data on the Y-axis, though, is not distinguished by different classes in this case.

Let's see how these two models compare against each other for classification purposes by running them against the familiar `iris` dataset. Begin by using PCA on the `iris` data and then look at the total variance attributed to each of the components, starting with using the `prcomp` function:

```
iris.pca <- prcomp(iris[, -5], center = T, scale. = T)
iris.pca$sdev^2/sum(iris.pca$sdev^2)

## [1] 0.729624454 0.228507618 0.036689219 0.005178709
```

Here, PCA informs you that you have basically two major components. Component 1 describes the variance of 72% of the data, and component 2 describes 23% of the variance in the data. These two vectors combined describe a good 96% of the data; you can ignore the other components for the time being (to keep the visualizations a bit simpler).

Before jumping headlong into LDA, we first need to establish what the *prior distribution* of data is. We briefly touched on this subject while discussing Bayesian statistics.

For a quick refresh, the prior distribution is the distribution of the data that you're modeling, essentially. In some cases, you don't know for sure what the distribution might be, but you do in this case. Because you are running a classification model on the `iris` data, the only class type of data that you have is related to the `Species` variable. You can see what the prior distribution would be in this case by looking at that specific variable:

```
table(iris$Species)
```

```
##
##     setosa versicolor  virginica
##         50         50         50
```

Here, there are three classes, all equally distributed. The prior distribution in this case would be (1/3) for each class. You need to specify this as a vector when training the LDA model. After you do that, you can look at how the LDA corollary to principal components compare by doing basically the same mathematical approach:

```
library(MASS)

iris.lda <- lda(Species ~ ., data = iris, prior = c(1/3, 1/3,
    1/3))
iris.lda$svd^2/sum(iris.lda$svd^2)
```

```
## [1] 0.991212605 0.008787395
```

The output here shows that there are two singular values, the first one describing a whopping 99% of the variance in the data and the other one a lowly 0.8%. If you want to see how the two linear discriminants are related to each of the features in the data in a similar fashion to how you did it with PCA, you can simply call the scalings:

```
iris.lda$scaling
```

```
##                    LD1         LD2
## Sepal.Length  0.8293776  0.02410215
## Sepal.Width   1.5344731  2.16452123
## Petal.Length -2.2012117 -0.93192121
## Petal.Width  -2.8104603  2.83918785
```

Next, you can do the usual confusion matrix to see how well the LDA model compares with the actual answers for the `iris` species data:

```
iris.lda.prediction <- predict(iris.lda, newdata = iris)

table(iris.lda.prediction$class, iris$Species)
```

```
##
##              setosa versicolor virginica
##   setosa         50          0         0
##   versicolor      0         48         1
##   virginica       0          2        49
```

The LDA model seems to be pretty spot-on. Next, you can try to visualize the difference between PCA and LDA. Let's recall the formulations with these two models. PCA is an unsupervised learner. We don't tell PCA to try to separate our data based on a certain class, it just goes about its business doing so. On the other hand, with LDA, we do need to specify a class by which to separate, and therefore the latter is a supervised model.

Supervised models will tend to be better at separating data than unsupervised ones. Figure 7-6 tests this by comparing the outputs from PCA compared to LDA:

```
combined <- data.frame(Species = iris[, "Species"], pca = iris.pca$x,
    lda = iris.lda.prediction$x)

library(ggplot2)

library(gridExtra)
lda.plot <- ggplot(combined) + geom_point(aes(lda.LD1, lda.LD2,
    shape = Species)) + scale_shape_manual(values = c(0, 1, 2))

pca.plot <- ggplot(combined) + geom_point(aes(pca.PC1, pca.PC2,
    shape = Species)) + scale_shape_manual(values = c(0, 1, 2))

grid.arrange(pca.plot, lda.plot)
```

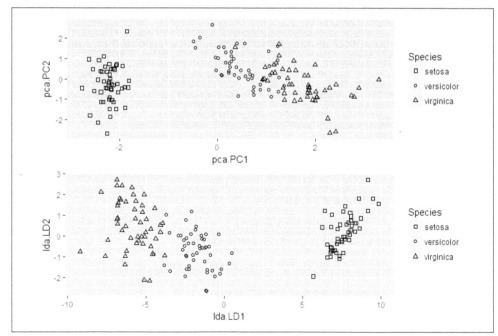

Figure 7-6. A comparison of PCA versus LDA

Figure 7-6 shows PCA on top and LDA on the bottom. The goal here is to see how well each model separates your data. In PCA, notice that the setosa data is well separated from the rest, but the versicolor data seems to have some overlap with the virginica data at around the pca.PC1=1.5 range. In comparison, LDA also separates the setosa data well, but it looks like it performs better at keeping the overlap between versicolor and virginica to a minimum.

Support Vector Machines

Support vector machines, known better as SVMs, are a machine learning model that use hyperplanes to separate data. To separate and partition our data, we find some kind of plane (or in the cases of two-dimensional data, a line) that separates them and use the vectors that maximize the separation in the data, as illustrated in Figure 7-7.

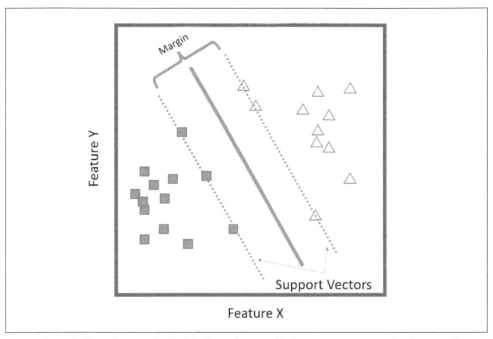

Figure 7-7. A plot of a simple SVM algorithm applied onto some example data; a plane, or a line, separates our data with two support vectors yielding the maximum distance of separation between the two types of data and the plane itself

SVMs work by employing something called the "kernel trick." This is a method by which we can transform the data for which we are trying to draw a decision boundary, and then apply a hyperplane separation on that transformed data.

For example, if we had data in a bull's eye, with a small clump surrounded by a ring, this would be impossible to separate by using a line or a two-dimensional surface.

Instead, if we transform the data into polar coordinates, we can then separate the data easily using a hyperplane. In practice, this transformation is more or less a black box because the feature space can be quite complex, but the idea is still the same.

In Figure 7-8, you can see the vectors that partition the data by coming back to our favorite iris dataset:

```
library("e1071")

s <- sample(150, 100)
col <- c("Petal.Length", "Petal.Width", "Species")
iris_train <- iris[s, col]
iris_test <- iris[-s, col]

svmfit <- svm(Species ~ ., data = iris_train, kernel = "linear",
    cost = 0.1, scale = FALSE)

plot(svmfit, iris_train[, col])
```

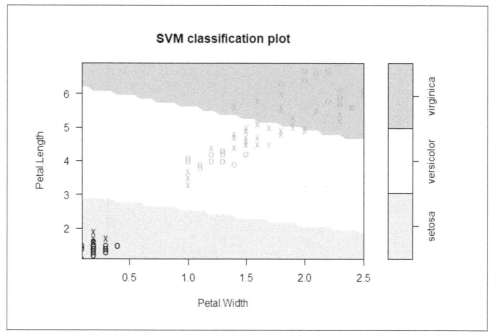

Figure 7-8. A plot of the data with SVM classification and boundaries overlaid

What we see as a result in Figure 7-8 are the classification boundaries as denoted by the SVM training model. It's pretty clear that the data in the lower left can be easily separated from the rest and be classified appropriately, but there might be some fine-tuning required to separate the versicolor and virginica data. The Xs on the plot show the support vectors and the bands show the predicted class regions.

You can use the tune function to help find the best cost parameter for optimal tuning with the SVM:

```
tuned <- tune(svm, Species ~ ., data = iris_train, kernel = "linear",
    ranges = list(cost = c(0.001, 0.01, 0.1, 1, 10, 100)))

summary(tuned)

##
## Parameter tuning of 'svm':
##
## - sampling method: 10-fold cross validation
##
## - best parameters:
##   cost
##      1
##
## - best performance: 0.04
##
## - Detailed performance results:
##     cost error dispersion
## 1 1e-03  0.70 0.09428090
## 2 1e-02  0.37 0.16363917
## 3 1e-01  0.05 0.05270463
## 4 1e+00  0.04 0.06992059
## 5 1e+01  0.05 0.07071068
## 6 1e+02  0.05 0.07071068
```

This reveals that the best cost parameter to use is 1, with which you can then rerun the model, as shown in Figure 7-9:

```
svmfit <- svm(Species ~ ., data = iris_train, kernel = "linear",
    cost = 1, scale = FALSE)

plot(svmfit, iris_train[, col])
```

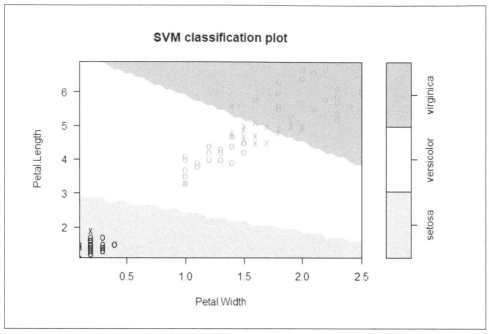

Figure 7-9. A tuned SVM will have a slightly better fit to the data than an untuned one

You can use SVM classification for nonlinear decision boundaries, as well. In earlier examples, you've seen how some machine learning algorithms separate data based only on straight lines. For example, logistic regression separates data using straight lines, and decision trees also separate data by using straight lines, but by drawing boxes around the data.

SVMs are useful because they can employ a method known as the "kernel trick" to transform our data, then perform operations on that transformed data. What this allows is for us to draw curves around our data instead of just straight lines in order to get better fits. The downside, however, comes with model explainability. Like neural networks, we can pass data through an SVM and get some meaningful output, but describing the process by which the transformations occur can often be swept under the moniker of a "black box" operation.

Let's take a look at Figure 7-10, which shows how you can employ SVMs to draw curved decision boundaries for classification. For this example, let's load the `cats` dataset from the MASS package:

```
plot(x = cats$Hwt, y = cats$Bwt, pch = as.numeric(cats$Sex))
```

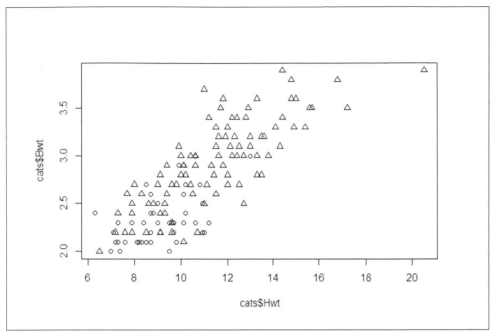

Figure 7-10. A plot of the cats data from the MASS package

At first glance, it looks like it will be tough to separate the male cats (triangles) from the female cats (circles). What you can do here is to run another SVM model on this data; this will automatically produce a nonlinear boundary that you can see in Figure 7-11:

```
library(MASS)
library(e1071)
data(cats)
model <- svm(Sex ~ ., data = cats)

print(model)

##
## Call:
## svm(formula = Sex ~ ., data = cats)
##
##
## Parameters:
##    SVM-Type:  C-classification
##  SVM-Kernel:  radial
##        cost:  1
##       gamma:  0.5
##
## Number of Support Vectors:  84
```

```
summary(model)

##
## Call:
## svm(formula = Sex ~ ., data = cats)
##
##
## Parameters:
##     SVM-Type:  C-classification
##   SVM-Kernel:  radial
##         cost:  1
##        gamma:  0.5
##
## Number of Support Vectors:  84
##
##   ( 39 45 )
##
##
## Number of Classes:  2
##
## Levels:
##   F M
```

```
plot(model, cats)
```

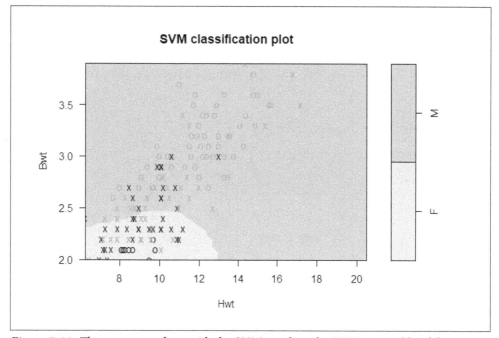

Figure 7-11. The same cats data with the SVM overlay; the SVM is capable of drawing a nonlinear classification boundary on the data, which can be useful when you're trying to create decision boundaries for data that overlaps

Finally, you can use SVM classification in the standard confusion matrix to see how well the data lines up:

```
data.samples <- sample(1:nrow(cats), nrow(cats) * 0.7, replace = FALSE)
training.data <- cats[data.samples, ]
test.data <- cats[-data.samples, ]

svm.cats <- svm(Sex ~ ., data = training.data)
prediction.svm <- predict(svm.cats, test.data[, -1], type = "class")

table(test.data[, 1], prediction.svm)

##      prediction.svm
##        F  M
##    F 10  7
##    M  6 21
```

k-Nearest Neighbors

k-nearest neighbors (kNN) is a rather simple machine learning algorithm that basically takes all the available cases in our data and predicts a target based on some kind of similarity measure—in this case, distance.

We can show how this works with a brief example. Suppose that I'm trying to find a new bike to fit me. Bikes come in a variety of configurations that can have very different measurements depending on the size and style of fit that I want. There might be 10 or more different measurements that describe the perfect fit for me. However, going to a bike shop and trying out different bikes takes time and I'd rather use a mathematical approach to guess how well a bike will fit without leaving my house.

Table 7-1 collects five measurements for a group of bikes from online manuals.

Table 7-1. Five measurements for a series of bikes

bike	m1	m2	m3	m4	m5
my bike	25	30	11.2	12	7
test1	27	34	7	12	8
test2	22	35	12	15	8
test3	18	39	9	24	8
test4	27	39	8	28	8
test5	29	34	8	24	8
test6	11	38	8	20	7
test7	25	31	10	12	8
test8	25	33	9	21	9
test9	26	34	14	23	7
test10	27	30	12	17	9

A very important step is to first normalize the values in the table. Doing so puts all the measurements on an equal playing field, so if some measurements are very small, they are not forgotten among the larger magnitude measurements. We do this by simply dividing each measurement by the sum of the measurements in that column, as illustrated in Table 7-2.

Table 7-2. Normalized bike measurements

bike	m1	m2	m3	m4	m5	fit	dist
my bike	0.0954	0.1145	0.0427	0.0458	0.0267	0.1639	0.0000
test1	0.1031	0.1298	0.0267	0.0458	0.0305	0.1766	0.0127
test2	0.0840	0.1336	0.0458	0.0573	0.0305	0.1766	0.0127
test3	0.0687	0.1489	0.0344	0.0916	0.0305	0.1933	0.0294
test4	0.1031	0.1489	0.0305	0.1069	0.0305	0.2146	0.0507
test5	0.1107	0.1298	0.0305	0.0916	0.0305	0.1984	0.0345
test6	0.0420	0.1450	0.0305	0.0763	0.0267	0.1740	0.0101
test7	0.0954	0.1183	0.0382	0.0458	0.0305	0.1661	0.0022
test8	0.0954	0.1260	0.0344	0.0802	0.0344	0.1837	0.0198
test9	0.0992	0.1298	0.0534	0.0878	0.0267	0.1948	0.0309
test10	0.1031	0.1145	0.0458	0.0649	0.0344	0.1767	0.0128

For each bike, there are measurements m1 through m5, a calculated field of fit and a simple distance dist. In kNN distance measuring, we use the Euclidean distance measurement given by the following:

$$d = \sqrt{(m1^2 + m2^2 + m3^2 + \ldots)}$$

This defines the fit field in Table 7-2. After we have the measurement for the bike's fit, we can see how far away from that baseline the bikes are by simply taking the difference between what bike we're interested in and the baseline. This is the dist value in the table. We then sort by dist and the value that's closest to the baseline is the nearest neighbor. If we wanted *k* bikes that were the best fit, maybe the top three, for example, we would simply take the top three bikes that aren't our baseline.

For a regression example, the kNN algorithm calculates the average of our response variable for the kNNs. The mathematical underpinnings are the same for classification, but tweaked slightly because those are categorical instead of numeric values.

Let's go through a simple example from the venerable mtcars dataset:

```
knn.ex <- head(mtcars[, 1:3])
knn.ex
```

```
##                      mpg cyl disp
## Mazda RX4           21.0   6  160
## Mazda RX4 Wag       21.0   6  160
## Datsun 710          22.8   4  108
## Hornet 4 Drive      21.4   6  258
## Hornet Sportabout   18.7   8  360
## Valiant             18.1   6  225
```

If you wanted to find the kNNs to the final row for the "Valiant" car based on the mpg feature, you would find what the Euclidean distance is between all the other features:

```
knn.ex$dist <- sqrt((knn.ex$cyl - 6)^2 + (knn.ex$disp - 225)^2)
knn.ex[order(knn.ex[, 4]), ]
```

```
##                      mpg cyl disp      dist
## Valiant             18.1   6  225    0.0000
## Hornet 4 Drive      21.4   6  258   33.0000
## Mazda RX4           21.0   6  160   65.0000
## Mazda RX4 Wag       21.0   6  160   65.0000
## Datsun 710          22.8   4  108  117.0171
## Hornet Sportabout   18.7   8  360  135.0148
```

This example takes the values for the "Valiant" car that aren't the feature you're trying to model and calculates the Euclidean distance between them. This example shows the five nearest neighbor data points based on the selected features.

Regression Using kNN

Figure 7-12 demonstrates running a regression model with the kNN algorithm:

```
library(caret)

data(BloodBrain)

inTrain <- createDataPartition(logBBB, p = 0.8)[[1]]

trainX <- bbbDescr[inTrain, ]
trainY <- logBBB[inTrain]

testX <- bbbDescr[-inTrain, ]
testY <- logBBB[-inTrain]

fit <- knnreg(trainX, trainY, k = 3)

plot(testY, predict(fit, testX))
```

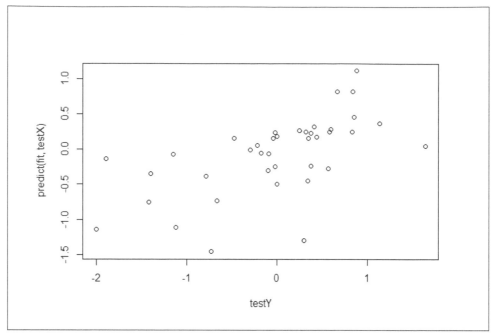

Figure 7-12. A plot of error estimation for the data from kNN regression

Classification Using kNN

Using kNN to perform classification works roughly the same way as with regression. In this example, you'll use the classification modeling system from the RWeka package. Because this modeling suite relies on Java, you need to know what version of R you're running; you can check this by calling the following function:

```
Sys.getenv("R_ARCH")
```

```
## [1] "/x64"
```

This example indicates a 64-bit architecture of R.

 I am also using the 64-bit version of Java, but more often than not, issues with this system come from a type mismatch in which, for example, you might have a 64-bit version of R installed but a 32-bit version of Java.

In any case, running the classification system from RWeka is rather simple and produces some nice outputs:

```
library(RWeka)
iris <- read.arff(system.file("arff", "iris.arff", package = "RWeka"))
```

```
classifier <- IBk(class ~ ., data = iris)
summary(classifier)

##
## === Summary ===
##
## Correctly Classified Instances       150               100     %
## Incorrectly Classified Instances       0                 0     %
## Kappa statistic                        1
## Mean absolute error                    0.0085
## Root mean squared error                0.0091
## Relative absolute error                1.9219 %
## Root relative squared error            1.9335 %
## Total Number of Instances            150
##
## === Confusion Matrix ===
##
##    a  b  c   <-- classified as
##   50  0  0 |  a = Iris-setosa
##    0 50  0 |  b = Iris-versicolor
##    0  0 50 |  c = Iris-virginica
```

Using the RWeka package, you can get all sorts of good information out without having to explicitly calculate it by hand. In this case, there's a lot of error types as well as a handy confusion matrix output all by just calling the summary of the object.

You can also evaluate the resultant RWeka object with some handy built-in cross-validation as given by the numFolds option:

```
classifier <- IBk(class ~ ., data = iris, control = Weka_control(K = 20,
    X = TRUE))

evaluate_Weka_classifier(classifier, numFolds = 10)

## === 10 Fold Cross Validation ===
##
## === Summary ===
##
## Correctly Classified Instances       143               95.3333 %
## Incorrectly Classified Instances       7                4.6667 %
## Kappa statistic                        0.93
## Mean absolute error                    0.046
## Root mean squared error                0.1653
## Relative absolute error               10.351  %
## Root relative squared error           35.0668 %
## Total Number of Instances            150
##
## === Confusion Matrix ===
##
##    a  b  c   <-- classified as
##   50  0  0 |  a = Iris-setosa
```

```
##    0 47  3 |  b = Iris-versicolor
##    0  4 46 |  c = Iris-virginica
```

Summary

In this chapter, we talked briefly about other machine learning models that you might encounter in the field. Naive Bayesian statistics models are ones that rely on a bold (hence, the naive part) assumption that all the features in our dataset are independent of one another. Although this might be true in some circumstances, in many cases there might be correlations within the data. In any case, naive Bayes models can work very well for certain purposes.

If you're concerned about unwanted correlations in your data, you can rely on principal component analysis (PCA). This is a technique that reformulates your data to be an amalgamation of a few components that explain most of the variation in the model. By representing the data this way, you can simplify inputs to machine learning models, but also use it as a compression technique. There are other types of component analysis, with linear discriminant analysis (LDA) being a strong competitor to traditional PCA.

Often, classification exercises rely on linear boundaries to classify data into certain groups. In this chapter, we demonstrated that you can use support vector machines (SVMs) as a linear classifier but also for nonlinear boundaries, as well. SVMs work based on passing the data through transformations known as a *kernel trick*, but can sometimes be complex enough to be essentially treated as a black box.

Finally, you looked at regression and classification techniques with *k*-nearest neighbor machine learning (kNN). This is an algorithm that relies on Euclidean distance ranking to other data points in order to make predictions. You take a baseline of data, measure the distance between all the points, and compare other data with it. The *k*-nearest data points are the values you get as a result. This handy algorithm is reasonably easy to explain and can be found in many packages throughout the R ecosystem, including the RWeka package.

## CHAPTER 8

Machine Learning with the caret Package

So far, we've been doing machine learning in a very ad hoc manner. We have some data, we want to fit a model to it, and then we tune the model to give us the best result based on whatever sampling processes we might have done and depending on how the data itself is organized. A lot of this relies on the ability to recognize when to use certain algorithms. Just by visualizing a set of data, we can usually determine whether we can slap a linear regression on it, if it makes sense. Likewise, we've seen examples for which data is better suited to be clustered via a kmeans algorithm or something similar.

One issue that we've seen is that a lot of these algorithms can be very different from one another. The options for the lm() function are quite different from that of the nnet() function. Surely there exists something that provides a common interface for all these different yet commonly used algorithms. We're in luck with R in that the caret package offers a powerhouse of tools for us to use to help streamline our model building.

The name "caret" is an acronym that stands for "Classification and Regression Training," but the package itself is capable of much more. In the R ecosystem, there are hundreds of machine learning packages. Becoming familiar with the quirks and special functionality for each one can be a daunting task. Lucky for us, caret provides a common interface for all of these packages. Caret also provides great functionality for splitting our data. It's trivial for us to split a data frame into a 70% train and a 30% test set, but for more complex ways of splitting the data and sampling it, such as stratified random sampling, caret provides a nice way to accomplish that. The caret package is also a robust system for feature selection. We can ask caret to help select which columns or features best suit the type of model we want to run. Finally, caret can help with a more streamlined way to tune our models. As previously mentioned, not only can some models be different in what options they take, but sometimes they can be horribly complicated. `caret` provides nice functionality for simplification without loss of robust model tuning capabilities.

The Titanic Dataset

In this chapter, we focus on seeing how `caret` helps when working on a famous dataset: that of the doomed ocean liner the *Titanic*, which sank in the North Atlantic Ocean in 1912. This dataset is often used in educational contexts for many reasons. It's a very well-known historical event, so most people dealing with the data already have some context as to the background for it. The *Titanic* dataset is also a good proxy for other types of commonly seen data in industry, such as data for customer profiles.

The goal for this chapter is to use the `caret` package to build a machine learning model in which you will try and predict whether someone survived their trip on the ill-fated ocean liner. You will build a model with the function form that we've seen earlier in this book written like `train(Survived ~ .)`, where you are modeling off the `Survived` parameter. However, to model from all of the other data that you're interested in, we might need to clean up and organize the data a bit better than its original form.

Let's explore the data at a top level to become better acquainted with it:

```
train <- read.csv("train.csv")
str(train)

## 'data.frame':    891 obs. of  12 variables:
## $ PassengerId: int  1 2 3 4 5 6 7 8 9 10 ...
## $ Survived   : int  0 1 1 1 0 0 0 0 1 1 ...
## $ Pclass     : int  3 1 3 1 3 1 3 1 3 2 ...
## $ Name       : Factor w/ 891 levels "Abbing, Mr. Anthony",..: 109 191 358
277 16 559 520 629 417 581 ...
## $ Sex        : Factor w/ 2 levels "female","male": 2 1 1 1 2 2 2 2 1 1 ...
## $ Age        : num  22 38 26 35 35 NA 54 2 27 14 ...
## $ SibSp      : int  1 1 0 1 0 0 0 3 0 1 ...
## $ Parch      : int  0 0 0 0 0 0 0 1 2 0 ...
## $ Ticket     : Factor w/ 681 levels "110152","110413",..: 524 597 670 50
473 276 86 396 345 133 ...
## $ Fare       : num  7.25 71.28 7.92 53.1 8.05 ...
## $ Cabin      : Factor w/ 148 levels "","A10","A14",..: 1 83 1 57 1 1 131 1
1 1 ...
## $ Embarked   : Factor w/ 4 levels "","C","Q","S": 4 2 4 4 4 3 4 4 4 2 ...
```

Some of this data might look like something you see in a typical customer churn analysis. There's a unique ID for each passenger; a binary value that indicates whether the passenger survived; what travel class they were on board (First, Second, or Third); personal information data in the form of name, gender, age; the number of siblings or spouses with whom they were traveling; number of parents or children with whom they were traveling; their ticket number; the ticket fare; cabin number; and point of embarkation (C is Cherbourg, Q is Queenstown, and S is Southampton).

Some of this data isn't very useful for the analysis you'll perform. Things like unique identifiers don't reveal anything about trends and only serve to conflate the models. PassengerId and Name we can forget about using in that case. The information in the ticket could be useful, but the formatting is a nightmare. Cabin data could be useful, but there are a lot of missing values. So for this exercise, let's set aside PassengerId, Name, Ticket, and Cabin.

Data Wrangling

There are some clean-up steps that you want to perform before unleashing your models on the data. Notice that the port of embarkation has a couple of blank values, Age has some NA values, and you might want to split up some of the data from SibSp and Parch into more coherent forms so that the model knows how to deal with that information better. Let's deal with the missing Embarked data first:

```
table(train$Embarked)
```

```
##
##       C   Q   S
##   2 168  77 644
```

In this code chunk, there are two blanks, 168 people embarked from Cherbourg, 77 people embarked from Queenstown, and 644 embarked from Southampton. Let's make an assumption (more formally known as an *imputation*) that those two blanks can be labeled as whatever the largest factor is for that variable. So in this case, you're assuming the blanks are from Southampton because most of the Embarked data points are, so it's probably a safe bet. If the data were more homogeneous, you would need to formulate a more complicated solution, as illustrated here:

```
train$Embarked[train$Embarked == ""] <- "S"
```

Now you've assigned those blanks to the value that has the most frequency. Up next, let's look at the ages in the data:

```
table(is.na(train$Age))[2]/table(is.na(train$Age))[1]
```

```
##      TRUE
## 0.2478992
```

```
summary(train$Age)
```

```
##    Min. 1st Qu.  Median    Mean 3rd Qu.    Max.    NA's
##    0.42   20.12   28.00   29.70   38.00   80.00     177
```

This code informs us that almost 25% of the Age data is missing. If you look at the summary statistics for that column, you could do the same process that you did before by simply replacing all the missing values with whatever the most frequent (in this case, the median) value is for that data. You would be reassigning every missing person's age to be 28 in that case, but intuitively that seems like you would be making a rather bold assumption. A safer bet would be to simply add a label if the age is missing for a given person and fill in that data later by using the power of caret:

```
train$is_age_missing <- ifelse(is.na(train$Age), 1, 0)
```

Now, consolidate the data that has the number of siblings and spouses (SibSp) and the parents and children (Parch) the person was traveling with into a total number of travelers. This will help with the model selection later on:

```
train$travelers <- train$SibSp + train$Parch + 1
```

Next, you need to factorize some of the data:

```
train$Survived <- as.factor(train$Survived)
train$Pclass <- as.factor(train$Pclass)
train$is_age_missing <- as.factor(train$is_age_missing)
```

Finally, you want to subset your data to just the features in which you're interested:

```
train2 <- subset(train, select = c(Survived, Pclass, Sex, Age,
    SibSp, Parch, Fare, Embarked, is_age_missing, travelers))
```

caret Unleashed

Now that we have the *Titanic* data in a cleaned-up form, it's time to begin using the caret package. R has many machine learning models built in or accessible via package download. However, the power with caret is that we can do much more than just simply training machine learning models. We can use caret as a data preprocessing tool to help with data imputation, we can use it to split our data into training and test sets, and we can leverage it for cross-validation techniques in addition to its great flexibility for model training.

Imputation

In this subsection, we're going to revisit the problem you saw earlier of having a lot of missing ages in the data. We hinted earlier that caret is good at figuring this out and, in fact, it supports many different methods of imputation. caret supports imputation by picking the median (similar to how you picked the values for the missing embark location earlier); it supports a method to impute based on *k*-nearest neighbors (kNN), which could be useful in other situations; and it supports imputation via bagged decision trees, which are similar enough in theory to random forests. In this case, you're going with the bagged decision trees because it's the most accurate method. Despite the computational heft of this method, this particular dataset is small enough that you can run this without a major time penalty.

The limitation with imputation in `caret` is that you need to change all of the factor variables into numeric data for the process to work correctly. For example, the `Embark` data is categorical with three values (C,Q,S); this needs to be transposed into numeric values. You might be tempted to relabel C to 0, Q to 1, and S to 2, but this would perform poorly with the model. Instead, you need to take that data and pivot it such that you have a column that is either 0 or 1 if its `Embark` is C, 0 or 1 if its `Embark` is Q, and likewise for S. This will be more obvious when you run the code:

```
library(caret)

dummy <- dummyVars(~., data = train2[, -1])
dummy_train <- predict(dummy, train2[, -1])
head(dummy_train)
```

```
##    Pclass.1 Pclass.2 Pclass.3 Sex.female Sex.male Age SibSp Parch    Fare
## 1         0        0        1          0        1  22     1     0  7.2500
## 2         1        0        0          1        0  38     1     0 71.2833
## 3         0        0        1          1        0  26     0     0  7.9250
## 4         1        0        0          1        0  35     1     0 53.1000
## 5         0        0        1          0        1  35     0     0  8.0500
## 6         0        0        1          0        1  NA     0     0  8.4583
##    Embarked. Embarked.C Embarked.Q Embarked.S is_age_missing.0
## 1         0          0          0          1                1
## 2         0          1          0          0                1
## 3         0          0          0          1                1
## 4         0          0          0          1                1
## 5         0          0          0          1                1
## 6         0          0          1          0                0
##    is_age_missing.1 travelers
## 1                 0         2
## 2                 0         2
## 3                 0         1
## 4                 0         2
## 5                 0         1
## 6                 1         1
```

This code splits the possible categorical values that `Pclass` could take (1,2,3) into separate columns that are a binary indicator if they were first class, second class, or third class. Likewise with the other categorical variables only. Amazingly, `caret` is smart enough to perform this functionality only on the factor variables, not the data that's already numeric. Now, all of our data is in a handy numerical form and makes more sense from a modeling standpoint.

The next step is to use the `preProcess` function. Notice that the preview still shows an NA value for one passenger; this is the step that fills in that value. The `preProcess` function is very powerful and offers more than 15 different methods to model the values you want, but let's stick with `bagImpute` for now:

```
pre.process <- preProcess(dummy_train, method = "bagImpute")
imputed.data <- predict(pre.process, dummy_train)
head(imputed.data)
```

```
##   Pclass.1 Pclass.2 Pclass.3 Sex.female Sex.male      Age SibSp Parch
## 1        0        0        1          0        1 22.00000     1     0
## 2        1        0        0          1        0 38.00000     1     0
## 3        0        0        1          1        0 26.00000     0     0
## 4        1        0        0          1        0 35.00000     1     0
## 5        0        0        1          0        1 35.00000     0     0
## 6        0        0        1          0        1 31.36861     0     0
##       Fare Embarked. Embarked.C Embarked.Q Embarked.S is_age_missing.0
## 1  7.2500         0          0          0          1                1
## 2 71.2833         0          1          0          0                1
## 3  7.9250         0          0          0          1                1
## 4 53.1000         0          0          0          1                1
## 5  8.0500         0          0          0          1                1
## 6  8.4583         0          0          1          0                0
##   is_age_missing.1 travelers
## 1                0         2
## 2                0         2
## 3                0         1
## 4                0         2
## 5                0         1
## 6                1         1
```

The single NA age that you had earlier has now been predicted via bagged decision trees to have an age of 28.96071. Great! All the NA values are now gone and replaced with numeric predictions. The last step is to take these predicted values and put those back into the original training set:

```
train$Age <- imputed.data[, 6]
head(train$Age, 20)
```

```
##  [1] 22.00000 38.00000 26.00000 35.00000 35.00000 31.36861 54.00000
##  [8]  2.00000 27.00000 14.00000  4.00000 58.00000 20.00000 39.00000
## [15] 14.00000 55.00000  2.00000 33.41508 31.00000 25.73630
```

At this point, you have some filled-in ages that were previously NAs, as denoted by the number of digits after the decimal. You've predicted ages of 28.96071, 33.02747, and 24.55931 for the first 20 entries in the data.

Data Splitting

Let's now see how you can use caret to split the data into training and test sets. If the dataset had close to 50% of survivors, we could do a simple random sample by just plucking out half the data on which to train. Instead, you need to do a stratified random sample because of the imbalance between those who survived and those who didn't. This next step will keep the proportions of the Survived feature the same across each of the stratified splits. You're instructing the createDataPartition function that you want this split to run only once, but in theory you could run it multiple times. You're taking 70% for training data, and, finally, the `list` option just gives you the row numbers of the partition that you can pass back into the training data to effectively split it:

```
set.seed(123)
partition_indexes <- createDataPartition(train$Survived, times = 1,
    p = 0.7, list = FALSE)
titanic.train <- train[partition_indexes, ]
titanic.test <- train[-partition_indexes, ]
```

caret Under the Hood

Before you jump into training models with `caret`, let's take a quick peek under the hood of the all the stuff you can play around with regarding model tuning. At the highest level, `caret` looks like this:

```
train.model <- train(Survived ~ ., data = titanic.train, method = "xgbTree",
    tuneGrid = tune.grid, trControl = train.control)
```

You likely see a similar form to other machine learning model training scenarios you looked at for which there is a response—in this case, `Survived` being modeled against all the other features in your dataset. Let's expand on the other features:

data

This one is pretty self-explanatory—it's the object from which you're getting your training data.

method

This is the specific machine learning algorithm that you want to deploy. The one you're using for the moment, `xgbTree`, is a form of extreme gradient boosted decision trees.

tuneGrid

This is a data frame of parameters that you can pass to your model training and have the model train and evaluate for those parameters and then move on to the next set of parameters. This is model dependent, but you'll see how you can better understand how to use it.

trControl

The train control options let you specify how you want to do cross-validation techniques for training.

Caret Methods in Focus

Let's dive a little deeper into the method. Here we can specify a specific machine learning algorithm to use for model training. The list of legal methods to use is colossal and is included in the appendix of this book. There are more than 200 methods that you can plug and play in here to change machine learning models on the fly. If we didn't want to worry about the tuning parameter grid, we could simply hot swap out `xgbTree` with `rf`, and now we are doing a random forest model. We could swap out `rf` with `nnet`, and now we're doing a neural network. It's almost shocking how easy `caret` makes trying out different machine learning algorithms!

Further, with our method of `xgbTree`, we can look at all the different inner workings going on by calling the `getModelInfo` function from `caret`:

```
getModelInfo("xgbTree")
```

There's a whole host of things buried inside each of the over 200 models available from `caret`. Some of these are just descriptive entries for the model, others are input components to each `caret` model, and some are optional:

`label`
> Name of the model—in this case, "eXtreme Gradient Boosting"

`library`
> The necessary libraries to run this model. `caret` prompts you to download the libraries if you don't already have them installed, and will load them on the fly if you do.

`type`
> Is the model capable of handling regression, classification, or both? In this case both, because we have "Both" as the output.

`parameters`
> This is a data frame of the parameters, parameter classes (i.e., numeric), and specific labels used to tune the model.

`grid`
> Function used to create the tuning grid, unless otherwise specified by the user.

`loop`
> Optional parameter that allows users to create multiple submodel predictions from the same object.

`fit`
> This is what actually fits the model.

`predict`
> Function for creating model predictions.

prob
> Where appropriate, this function creates class probabilities.

predictors
> Optional function that returns the names of the features we used as our predictors in our model.

varImp
> Optional function that calculates variable importance.

levels
> Optional function, typically used for classification models that use a specific S4 method.

tags
> Descriptive entries on what the model is specifically capable of. Here we have the tags: "tree-based model, boosting, ensemble model, implicit feature selection."

sort
> Function that sorts the parameter by decreasing order of complexity.

Diving deeper into the `parameters` field, you can see all the different ways that you can tune this specific model:

```
xgb.params <- getModelInfo("xgbTree")
xgb.params$xgbTree$parameters
```

```
##            parameter    class                               label
## 1            nrounds  numeric                # Boosting Iterations
## 2          max_depth  numeric                      Max Tree Depth
## 3                eta  numeric                           Shrinkage
## 4              gamma  numeric              Minimum Loss Reduction
## 5   colsample_bytree  numeric         Subsample Ratio of Columns
## 6   min_child_weight  numeric Minimum Sum of Instance Weight
```

We can compare the tuning parameters for different models, as well:

```
nnet.params <- getModelInfo("nnet")
nnet.params$nnet$parameters
```

```
##  parameter    class         label
## 1      size  numeric #Hidden Units
## 2     decay  numeric  Weight Decay
```

This wealth of information teaches us not only what a new and potentially unfamiliar algorithm is capable of, but how it works at the code level and how best to tune it for optimal results.

Model Training

Finally, we can get to the actual meat of the model building. You first need to specify what training controls to pass to the model. Basically, you're telling `caret` how you want the model built. The key point here is that the process for training the model is actually independent of whatever model you select! You're telling `caret` that you'd like to do 10-fold cross-validation, repeated three times, and then go through a grid search. A grid search is when you go through a collection of parameters and choose the optimal ones. Essentially, this is making 30 pseudo-models and selecting the parameters that correspond to the best one; here's how to do it:

```
train.control <- trainControl(method = "repeatedcv", number = 10,
    repeats = 3, search = "grid")
```

In the following code, the `expand.grid()` function creates all of the permutations of all the values passed into it and creates a unique row for each permutation:

```
tune.grid <- expand.grid(eta = c(0.05, 0.075, 0.1),
                         nrounds = c(50, 75, 100),
                         max_depth = 6:8,
                         min_child_weight = c(2.0, 2.25, 2.5),
                         colsample_bytree = c(0.3, 0.4, 0.5),
                         gamma = 0
                         #subsample = 1
                         )
head(tune.grid)
```

```
##       eta nrounds max_depth min_child_weight colsample_bytree gamma
## 1 0.050      50        6                2              0.3      0
## 2 0.075      50        6                2              0.3      0
## 3 0.100      50        6                2              0.3      0
## 4 0.050      75        6                2              0.3      0
## 5 0.075      75        6                2              0.3      0
## 6 0.100      75        6                2              0.3      0
```

The resultant data frame has 243 combinations of the values you put into the `expand.grid()` function. You're asking `caret` to run 10-fold cross-validation three times on each of these values that you pass into the algorithm. Thus, now you're actually training 7,290 different models! That's going to take forever to compute, right?

As it happens, there's a nice package for parallelizing R code to make things like this run faster. From the doSnow package, you can use a function that will run several instances of R all at the same time with your code. The `registerDoSnow()` function tells `caret` that it can now use the available clusters for processing:

```
library(doSNOW)
cl <- makeCluster(3, type = "SOCK")
registerDoSNOW(cl)
```

Now for actually using `caret` for training. Here you have a similar structure to what you've seen in previous algorithms. You are taking the response variable, `Survived`, and modeling all the other factors against it. You are using an `xg-boost` algorithm in particular and having it iterate over all the different permutations of tuning parameters given by the grid that you expanded earlier. Finally, you're instructing it to use the training controls of 10-fold cross-validation and doing it three times. You then stop the parallelized cluster setup to save computational resources, given that you're done with the exhaustive training procedure:

```
caret.cv <- train(Survived ~ ., data = titanic.train, method = "xgbTree",
    tuneGrid = tune.grid, trControl = train.control)
stopCluster(cl)
```

Here are the results:

```
caret.cv
```

```
> caret.cv
extreme Gradient Boosting

625 samples
 13 predictor
  2 classes: '0', '1'

No pre-processing
Resampling: Cross-Validated (10 fold, repeated 3 times)
Summary of sample sizes: 563, 563, 562, 563, 562, 562, ...
Resampling results across tuning parameters:

  eta    max_depth  colsample_bytree  min_child_weight  nrounds  Accuracy   Kappa
  0.050  6          0.3               2.00               50      0.8031405  0.5651156
  0.050  6          0.3               2.00               75      0.8074074  0.5765204
  0.050  6          0.3               2.00              100      0.8089435  0.5813304
  0.050  6          0.3               2.25               50      0.8121778  0.5862264
  0.050  6          0.3               2.25               75      0.8079024  0.5786605
  0.050  6          0.3               2.25              100      0.8036269  0.5699862
```

This displays the results for each one of the combinations of modeling outputs. There's so much outputted to the console that a lot ends up being truncated from view, but the take-home message is at the end:

```
  0.075  8          0.3               2.25               50      0.8020055  0.5657020
  0.075  8          0.3               2.25               75      0.8036184  0.5715806
  0.075  8          0.3               2.25              100      0.7988138  0.5628455
  0.075  8          0.3               2.50               50      0.8030978  0.5686452
[ reached getOption("max.print") -- omitted 101 rows ]

Tuning parameter 'gamma' was held constant at a value of 0
Accuracy was used to select the optimal model using the largest value.
The final values used for the model were nrounds = 50, max_depth = 6, eta = 0.05,
 gamma = 0, colsample_bytree = 0.3 and min_child_weight = 2.25.
```

This says in order to select the optimal values for modeling, here are the `xg-boost` hyperparameters (from the earlier grid expand exercise) that work the best. Now that you have your trained model object, you can pass that into a prediction function to model the likelihood that someone survived the *Titanic* disaster:

```
preds <- predict(caret.cv, titanic.test)
```

Finally, you assess the model's capability by running it through a confusion matrix to see how well it will work with brand-new data:

```
confusionMatrix(preds, titanic.test$Survived)

## Confusion Matrix and Statistics
##
##              Reference
## Prediction    0    1
##           0  151   32
##           1   13   70
##
##                  Accuracy : 0.8308
##                    95% CI : (0.7803, 0.8738)
##       No Information Rate : 0.6165
##       P-Value [Acc > NIR] : 2.211e-14
##
##                     Kappa : 0.6292
##  Mcnemar's Test P-Value : 0.00729
##
##               Sensitivity : 0.9207
##               Specificity : 0.6863
##            Pos Pred Value : 0.8251
##            Neg Pred Value : 0.8434
##                Prevalence : 0.6165
##            Detection Rate : 0.5677
##      Detection Prevalence : 0.6880
##         Balanced Accuracy : 0.8035
##
##           'Positive' Class : 0
##
```

The `confusionMatrix` function provided by `caret` is very powerful. It provides a whole host of statistical information that you can use to determine model accuracy, not only for classification, but for regression problems as well. Step by step, you begin with an actual confusion matrix. The correct values predicted by the model are on the diagonal, so in this case it predicted correctly 153 values of the data that were Survived=0, but incorrectly predicted 29 of them. Likewise, with the other value of Survived=1 for which it predicted 73 correct values and 11 incorrect ones. The accuracy was about 85%, which is not bad.

Output from this function are also sensitivity and specificity. Sensitivity, in this case, is simply the correctly predicted 'Positive' Class out of the total number, so 153/(153+11), which gives 0.9329. What that means in English is that 93% of the time, you can correctly predict whether someone died on the *Titanic*. Similarly, specificity is the other column of data in the confusion matrix, which would be calculated like 73/(73+29) and gives 0.7157. This is predicting how accurately someone lived or not. What this tells you is that you need to do more diligence in terms of finding some features that better predict how people survived the *Titanic*, given that the model is already pretty accurate at predicting whether they died.

Comparing Multiple caret Models

So far, you've run one machine learning algorithm (extreme gradient boosted decision trees) on the *Titanic* data and achieved a pretty decent result. caret makes it very easy to plug and play different machine learning algorithms so that you can compare and contrast the results. Suppose that you want to compare how well a random forest and a neural network fare in terms of accuracy. All you would need to do is just replace "xgboost" with "rf". For the moment, ignore the specific tuning grid parameters and just run it normally:

```
cl <- makeCluster(3, type="SOCK")
registerDoSNOW(cl)

caret.rf <- train(Survived ~ .,
                  data = titanic.train,
                  method = "rf",
                  #tuneGrid = tune.grid,
                  trControl = train.control)

stopCluster(cl)

confusionMatrix(predict(caret.rf, titanic.test), titanic.test$Survived)

## Confusion Matrix and Statistics
##
##           Reference
## Prediction   0   1
##          0 151  39
##          1  13  63
##
##                Accuracy : 0.8045
##                  95% CI : (0.7517, 0.8504)
##     No Information Rate : 0.6165
##     P-Value [Acc > NIR] : 3.037e-11
##
##                   Kappa : 0.5656
##  Mcnemar's Test P-Value : 0.0005265
##
##             Sensitivity : 0.9207
##             Specificity : 0.6176
##          Pos Pred Value : 0.7947
##          Neg Pred Value : 0.8289
##              Prevalence : 0.6165
##          Detection Rate : 0.5677
##    Detection Prevalence : 0.7143
##       Balanced Accuracy : 0.7692
##
```

```
##         'Positive' Class : 0
##
```

The accuracy here, without any specific tuning done, is 80%. Not bad for just a simple change of a few characters in the training model. The xgboost model yielded 85% accuracy, and that was after a lengthy tuning process. Suppose that you want to run a generalized linear model, instead. You can run the same logic with that by providing glm as your algorithm of choice:

```
cl <- makeCluster(3, type="SOCK")
registerDoSNOW(cl)

caret.nnet <- train(Survived ~ .,
                    data = titanic.train,
                    method = "glm",
                    #tuneGrid = tune.grid,
                    trControl = train.control)

stopCluster(cl)

confusionMatrix(predict(caret.nnet, titanic.test), titanic.test$Survived)

## Confusion Matrix and Statistics
##
##           Reference
## Prediction   0   1
##         0 107  38
##         1  57  64
##
##                Accuracy : 0.6429
##                  95% CI : (0.5821, 0.7004)
##     No Information Rate : 0.6165
##     P-Value [Acc > NIR] : 0.20669
##
##                   Kappa : 0.2704
##  Mcnemar's Test P-Value : 0.06478
##
##             Sensitivity : 0.6524
##             Specificity : 0.6275
##          Pos Pred Value : 0.7379
##          Neg Pred Value : 0.5289
##              Prevalence : 0.6165
##          Detection Rate : 0.4023
##    Detection Prevalence : 0.5451
##       Balanced Accuracy : 0.6399
##
##        'Positive' Class : 0
##
```

The accuracy output for this is not so good, but you could likely solve that issue by fine-tuning your grid parameters.

Summary

We've covered a lot in this chapter about the machine learning package in R called caret. While its name stands for "Classification and Regression Training," you learned that caret is capable of much more. In particular, you saw how you can use it for data imputation, data splitting and sampling, and, finally, for model training.

Model training in caret is a breeze and very simple. We used the following form:

```
caret.cv <- train(Survived ~ ., data = titanic.train, method = "xgbTree",
    tuneGrid = tune.grid, trControl = train.control)
```

You were able to see the results of the training exercise by looking at the output training object—in this case, caret.cv. In that training object, you could see the results for accuracy based on all the input tuning parameters that you ran with the data. There was a lot of output, but the training object is smart enough to select the grouping of training parameters that yields the best accuracy for use in predictive parts of your workflow.

Finally, you took the training object and passed it through the predict() function and then passed that predicted result through caret's confusionMatrix() function. Using the specific confusionMatrix() function from caret is great because not only do you get the actual confusion matrix itself, but you get a whole host of other information shot out directly to the screen without any manual processing. You achieve accuracy, a 95% confidence interval, sensitivity, specificity, and many other statistical benchmarks against which you can compare just how well the model performed.

caret's design makes it very easy to switch what algorithm you use, as well. By simply chaining the xgbTree value in the train() function to something like rf for a random forest or glm for a generalized linear model, you can cover an entire range of machine learning models in a short period of time, without having to learn the intense intricacies of every model.

caret offers a dizzying number of models to choose from, though. Figuring out which one to use first is totally dependent on the data and the data scientist at the helm. This book includes an appendix that, using model information from caret, details each machine learning method available to use, if it's usable for classification, regression, or both, what the function call is to use it specifically, and some keywords that describe its functionality.

Encyclopedia of Machine Learning Models in caret

Although this list is long, it is by no means completely comprehensive. These are machine learning algorithms that we use with the caret package discussed in this book in more detail. One of the major powers of caret is that it gives you the ability to switch very quickly from using, for example, a random forest machine learning algorithm to a neural network. With caret, all we would need to do is change rf in our model to nnet. This appendix provides a reference to look up all of the available machine learning algorithm calls, what libraries they depend on, an overall description or label, and their model type (regression, classification, or both).

Table A-1. Machine learning algorithms in caret

Algorithm name	Library dependencies	Label	Type
ada	ada, plyr	Boosted Classification Trees	Classification
AdaBag	adabag, plyr	Bagged AdaBoost	Classification
AdaBoost.M1	adabag, plyr	AdaBoost.M1	Classification
adaboost	fastAdaboost	AdaBoost Classification Trees	Classification
amdai	adaptDA	Adaptive-Mixture Discriminant Analysis	Classification
ANFIS	frbs	Adaptive-Network-Based Fuzzy Inference System	Regression
avNNet	nnet	Model-Averaged Neural Network	Both
awnb	bnclassify	Naive Bayes Classifier with Attribute Weighting	Classification
awtan	bnclassify	Tree-Augmented Naive Bayes Classifier with Attribute Weighting	Classification
bag	caret	Bagged Model	Both
bagEarth	earth	Bagged MARS	Both
bagEarthGCV	earth	Bagged MARS using gCV Pruning	Both
bagFDA	earth, mda	Bagged-Flexible Discriminant Analysis	Classification

Algorithm name	Library dependencies	Label	Type
bagFDAGCV	earth	Bagged FDA using gCV Pruning	Classification
bartMachine	bartMachine	Bayesian Additive Regression Trees	Both
bayesglm	arm	Bayesian Generalized Linear Model	Both
bdk	kohonen	Self-Organizing Map	Both
binda	binda	Binary Discriminant Analysis	Classification
blackboost	party, mboost, plyr	Boosted Tree	Both
blasso	monomvn	The Bayesian lasso	Regression
blassoAveraged	monomvn	Bayesian Ridge Regression (Model Averaged)	Regression
Boruta	Boruta, randomForest	Random Forest with Additional Feature Selection	Both
bridge	monomvn	Bayesian Ridge Regression	Regression
brnn	brnn	Bayesian Regularized Neural Networks	Regression
BstLm	bst, plyr	Boosted Linear Model	Both
bstSm	bst, plyr	Boosted Smoothing Spline	Both
bstTree	bst, plyr	Boosted Tree	Both
C5.0	C50, plyr	C5.0	Classification
C5.0Cost	C50, plyr	Cost-Sensitive C5.0	Classification
C5.0Rules	C50	Single C5.0 Ruleset	Classification
C5.0Tree	C50	Single C5.0 Tree	Classification
cforest	party	Conditional Inference Random Forest	Both
chaid	CHAID	Chi-squared Automated Interaction Detection	Classification
CSimca	rrcovHD	SIMCA	Classification
ctree	party	Conditional Inference Tree	Both
ctree2	party	Conditional Inference Tree	Both
cubist	Cubist	Cubist	Regression
dda	sparsediscrim	Diagonal Discriminant Analysis	Classification
deepboost	deepboost	DeepBoost	Classification
DENFIS	frbs	Dynamic Evolving Neural-Fuzzy Inference System	Regression
dnn	deepnet	Stacked AutoEncoder Deep Neural Network	Both
dwdLinear	kerndwd	Linear Distance Weighted Discrimination	Classification
dwdPoly	kerndwd	Distance-Weighted Discrimination with Polynomial Kernel	Classification
dwdRadial	kernlab, kerndwd	Distance-Weighted Discrimination with Radial Basis Function Kernel	Classification
earth	earth	Multivariate Adaptive Regression Spline	Both
elm	elmNN	Extreme Learning Machine	Both
enet	elasticnet	Elasticnet	Regression
enpls.fs	enpls	Ensemble Partial Least Squares Regression with Feature Selection	Regression
enpls	enpls	Ensemble Partial Least Squares Regression	Regression
evtree	evtree	Tree Models from Genetic Algorithms	Both

Algorithm name	Library dependencies	Label	Type
extraTrees	extraTrees	Random Forest by Randomization	Both
fda	earth, mda	Flexible Discriminant Analysis	Classification
FH.GBML	frbs	Fuzzy Rules Using Genetic Cooperative-Competitive Learning and Pittsburgh	Classification
FIR.DM	frbs	Fuzzy Inference Rules by Descent Method	Regression
foba	foba	Ridge Regression with Variable Selection	Regression
FRBCS.CHI	frbs	Fuzzy Rules Using Chi's Method	Classification
FRBCS.W	frbs	Fuzzy Rules with Weight Factor	Classification
FS.HGD	frbs	Simplified TSK Fuzzy Rules	Regression
gam	mgcv	Generalized Additive Model using Splines	Both
gamboost	mboost, plyr	Boosted Generalized Additive Model	Both
gamLoess	gam	Generalized Additive Model using LOESS	Both
gamSpline	gam	Generalized Additive Model using Splines	Both
gausprLinear	kernlab	Gaussian Process	Both
gausprPoly	kernlab	Gaussian Process with Polynomial Kernel	Both
gausprRadial	kernlab	Gaussian Process with Radial Basis Function Kernel	Both
gbm	gbm, plyr	Stochastic Gradient Boosting	Both
gcvEarth	earth	Multivariate Adaptive Regression Splines	Both
GFS.FR.MOGUL	frbs	Fuzzy Rules via MOGUL	Regression
GFS.GCCL	frbs	Fuzzy Rules Using Genetic Cooperative-Competitive Learning	Classification
GFS.LT.RS	frbs	Genetic Lateral Tuning and Rule Selection of Linguistic Fuzzy Systems	Regression
GFS.THRIFT	frbs	Fuzzy Rules via Thrift	Regression
glm	native	Generalized Linear Model	Both
glmboost	plyr, mboost	Boosted Generalized Linear Model	Both
glmnet	glmnet	glmnet	Both
glmStepAIC	MASS	Generalized Linear Model with Stepwise Feature Selection	Both
gpls	gpls	Generalized Partial Least Squares	Classification
hda	hda	Heteroscedastic Discriminant Analysis	Classification
hdda	HDclassif	High-Dimensional Discriminant Analysis	Classification
hdrda	sparsediscrim	High-Dimensional Regularized Discriminant Analysis	Classification
HYFIS	frbs	Hybrid Neural Fuzzy Inference System	Regression
icr	fastICA	Independent Component Regression	Regression
J48	RWeka	C4.5-like Trees	Classification
JRip	RWeka	Rule-Based Classifier	Classification
kernelpls	pls	Partial Least Squares	Both
kknn	kknn	k-Nearest Neighbors	Both
knn	native	k-Nearest Neighbors	Both

Algorithm name	Library dependencies	Label	Type
krlsPoly	KRLS	Polynomial Kernel Regularized Least Squares	Regression
krlsRadial	KRLS, kernlab	Radial-Basis Function Kernel Regularized Least Squares	Regression
lars	lars	Least Angle Regression	Regression
lars2	lars	Least Angle Regression	Regression
lasso	elasticnet	The lasso	Regression
lda	MASS	Linear Discriminant Analysis	Classification
lda2	MASS	Linear Discriminant Analysis	Classification
leapBackward	leaps	Linear Regression with Backwards Selection	Regression
leapForward	leaps	Linear Regression with Forward Selection	Regression
leapSeq	leaps	Linear Regression with Stepwise Selection	Regression
Linda	rrcov	Robust Linear Discriminant Analysis	Classification
lm	native	Linear Regression	Regression
lmStepAIC	MASS	Linear Regression with Stepwise Selection	Regression
LMT	RWeka	Logistic Model Trees	Classification
loclda	klaR	Localized Linear Discriminant Analysis	Classification
logicBag	logicFS	Bagged Logic Regression	Both
LogitBoost	caTools	Boosted Logistic Regression	Classification
logreg	LogicReg	Logic Regression	Both
lssvmLinear	kernlab	Least Squares Support Vector Machine	Classification
lssvmPoly	kernlab	Least Squares Support Vector Machine with Polynomial Kernel	Classification
lssvmRadial	kernlab	Least Squares Support Vector Machine with Radial Basis Function Kernel	Classification
lvq	class	Learning Vector Quantization	Classification
M5	RWeka	Model Tree	Regression
M5Rules	RWeka	Model Rules	Regression
manb	bnclassify	Model Averaged Naive Bayes Classifier	Classification
mda	mda	Mixture Discriminant Analysis	Classification
Mlda	HiDimDA	Maximum Uncertainty Linear Discriminant Analysis	Classification
mlp	RSNNS	Multilayer Perceptron	Both
mlpML	RSNNS	Multilayer Perceptron, with multiple layers	Both
mlpSGD	FCNN4R	Multilayer Perceptron Network by Stochastic Gradient Descent	Regression
mlpWeightDecay	RSNNS	Multilayer Perceptron	Both
mlpWeightDecayML	RSNNS	Multilayer Perceptron, multiple layers	Both
multinom	nnet	Penalized Multinomial Regression	Classification
nb	klaR	Naive Bayes	Classification
nbDiscrete	bnclassify	Naive Bayes Classifier	Classification
nbSearch	bnclassify	Semi-Naive Structure Learner Wrapper	Classification
neuralnet	neuralnet	Neural Network	Regression

Algorithm name	Library dependencies	Label	Type
nnet	nnet	Neural Network	Both
nnls	nnls	Non-Negative Least Squares	Regression
nodeHarvest	nodeHarvest	Tree-Based Ensembles	Both
oblique.tree	oblique.tree	Oblique Trees	Classification
OneR	RWeka	Single-Rule Classification	Classification
ordinalNet	ordinalNet, plyr	Penalized Ordinal Regression	Both
ORFlog	obliqueRF	Oblique Random Forest	Classification
ORFpls	obliqueRF	Oblique Random Forest	Classification
ORFridge	obliqueRF	Oblique Random Forest	Classification
ORFsvm	obliqueRF	Oblique Random Forest	Classification
ownn	snn	Optimal-Weighted Nearest Neighbor Classifier	Classification
pam	pamr	Nearest Shrunken Centroids	Classification
parRF	e1071, randomForest, foreach	Parallel Random Forest	Both
PART	RWeka	Rule-Based Classifier	Classification
partDSA	partDSA	partDSA	Both
pcaNNet	nnet	Neural Networks with Feature Extraction	Both
pcr	pls	Principal Component Analysis	Regression
pda	mda	Penalized Discriminant Analysis	Classification
pda2	mda	Penalized Discriminant Analysis	Classification
penalized	penalized	Penalized Linear Regression	Regression
PenalizedLDA	penalizedLDA, plyr	Penalized Linear Discriminant Analysis	Classification
plr	stepPlr	Penalized Logistic Regression	Classification
pls	pls	Partial Least Squares	Both
plsRglm	plsRglm	Partial Least Squares Generalized Linear Models	Both
polr	MASS	Ordered Logistic or Probit Regression	Classification
ppr	native	Projection Pursuit Regression	Regression
protoclass	proxy, protoclass	Greedy Prototype Selection	Classification
pythonKnnReg	rPython	Knn regression via sklearn.neighbors.KNeighborsRegressor	Regression
qda	MASS	Quadratic Discriminant Analysis	Classification
QdaCov	rrcov	Robust Quadratic Discriminant Analysis	Classification
qrf	quantregForest	Quantile Random Forest	Regression
qrnn	qrnn	Quantile Regression Neural Network	Regression
randomGLM	randomGLM	Ensembles of Generalized Linear Models	Both
ranger	e1071, ranger	Random Forest	Both
rbf	RSNNS	Radial-Basis Function Network	Both
rbfDDA	RSNNS	Radial-Basis Function Network	Both
Rborist	Rborist	Random Forest	Both

Algorithm name	Library dependencies	Label	Type
rda	klaR	Regularized Discriminant Analysis	Classification
relaxo	relaxo, plyr	Relaxed Lasso	Regression
rf	randomForest	Random Forest	Both
rFerns	rFerns	Random Ferns	Classification
RFlda	HiDimDA	Factor-Based Linear Discriminant Analysis	Classification
rfRules	randomForest, inTrees, plyr	Random Forest Rule-Based Model	Both
ridge	elasticnet	Ridge Regression	Regression
rlda	sparsediscrim	Regularized Linear Discriminant Analysis	Classification
rlm	MASS	Robust Linear Model	Regression
rmda	robustDA	Robust Mixture Discriminant Analysis	Classification
rocc	rocc	ROC-Based Classifier	Classification
rotationForest	rotationForest	Rotation Forest	Classification
rotationForestCp	rpart, plyr, rotationForest	Rotation Forest	Classification
rpart	rpart	CART	Both
rpart1SE	rpart	CART	Both
rpart2	rpart	CART	Both
rpartCost	rpart	Cost-Sensitive CART	Classification
rpartScore	rpartScore, plyr	CART or Ordinal Responses	Classification
rqlasso	rqPen	Quantile Regression with LASSO penalty	Regression
rqnc	rqPen	Non-Convex Penalized Quantile Regression	Regression
RRF	randomForest, RRF	Regularized Random Forest	Both
RRFglobal	RRF	Regularized Random Forest	Both
rrlda	rrlda	Robust Regularized Linear Discriminant Analysis	Classification
RSimca	rrcovHD	Robust SIMCA	Classification
rvmLinear	kernlab	Relevance Vector Machines with Linear Kernel	Regression
rvmPoly	kernlab	Relevance Vector Machines with Polynomial Kernel	Regression
rvmRadial	kernlab	Relevance Vector Machines with Radial Basis Function Kernel	Regression
SBC	frbs	Subtractive Clustering and Fuzzy c-Means Rules	Regression
sda	sda	Shrinkage Discriminant Analysis	Classification
sddaLDA	SDDA	Stepwise Diagonal Linear Discriminant Analysis	Classification
sddaQDA	SDDA	Stepwise Diagonal Quadratic Discriminant Analysis	Classification
sdwd	sdwd	Sparse Distance Weighted Discrimination	Classification
simpls	pls	Partial Least Squares	Both
SLAVE	frbs	Fuzzy Rules Using the Structural Learning Algorithm on Vague Environment	Classification
slda	ipred	Stabilized Linear Discriminant Analysis	Classification

Algorithm name	Library dependencies	Label	Type
smda	sparseLDA	Sparse Mixture Discriminant Analysis	Classification
snn	snn	Stabilized Nearest Neighbor Classifier	Classification
sparseLDA	sparseLDA	Sparse Linear Discriminant Analysis	Classification
spikeslab	spikeslab, plyr	Spike and Slab Regression	Regression
spls	spls	Sparse Partial Least Squares	Both
stepLDA	klaR, MASS	Linear Discriminant Analysis with Stepwise Feature Selection	Classification
stepQDA	klaR, MASS	Quadratic Discriminant Analysis with Stepwise Feature Selection	Classification
superpc	superpc	Supervised Principal Component Analysis	Regression
svmBoundrange String	kernlab	Support Vector Machines with Boundrange String Kernel	Both
svmExpoString	kernlab	Support Vector Machines with Exponential String Kernel	Both
svmLinear	kernlab	Support Vector Machines with Linear Kernel	Both
svmLinear2	e1071	Support Vector Machines with Linear Kernel	Both
svmLinearWeights	e1071	Linear Support Vector Machines with Class Weights	Classification
svmPoly	kernlab	Support Vector Machines with Polynomial Kernel	Both
svmRadial	kernlab	Support Vector Machines with Radial Basis Function Kernel	Both
svmRadialCost	kernlab	Support Vector Machines with Radial Basis Function Kernel	Both
svmRadialSigma	kernlab	Support Vector Machines with Radial Basis Function Kernel	Both
svmRadialWeights	kernlab	Support Vector Machines with Class Weights	Classification
svmSpectrumString	kernlab	Support Vector Machines with Spectrum String Kernel	Both
tan	bnclassify	Tree-Augmented Naive Bayes Classifier	Classification
tanSearch	bnclassify	Tree-Augmented Naive Bayes Classifier Structure Learner Wrapper	Classification
treebag	ipred, plyr, e1071	Bagged CART	Both
vbmpRadial	vbmp	Variational Bayesian Multinomial Probit Regression	Classification
vglmAdjCat	VGAM	Adjacent Categories Probability Model for Ordinal Data	Classification
vglmContRatio	VGAM	Continuation Ratio Model for Ordinal Data	Classification
vglmCumulative	VGAM	Cumulative Probability Model for Ordinal Data	Classification
widekernelpls	pls	Partial Least Squares	Both
WM	frbs	Wang and Mendel Fuzzy Rules	Regression
wsrf	wsrf	Weighted Subspace Random Forest	Classification
xgbLinear	xgboost	eXtreme Gradient Boosting	Both
xgbTree	xgboost, plyr	eXtreme Gradient Boosting	Both
xyf	kohonen	Self-Organizing Maps	Both

Index

About the Author

Scott V. Burger is a senior data scientist who lives and works in Seattle. His programming experience comes from the realm of astrophysics, but he uses it in many different types of scenarios, ranging from business intelligence to database optimizations. Scott has built a solid career on explaining terse scientific concepts to the general public and wants to use that expertise to shed light on the world of machine learning for the general R user.

Colophon

The animal on the cover of *Introduction to Machine Learning with R* is an Australian raven (*Corvus coronoides*), an intelligent bird with glossy black feathers and (as an adult) striking white eyes. It is sometimes casually referred to as a crow, though this raven is distinguishable from Australian crow species due to its fluffy throat hackles. There is no consistent distinction between crows and ravens, though in general, crows are categorized as such based on their smaller size. The Australian raven is found in the southern and eastern regions of the continent—its natural habitat is woodland, but it has adapted readily to life in urban areas.

The Australian raven is omnivorous (though it tends to eat more meat), with a diet of fruit, insects, eggs, carrion, small animals, and grains. It's also opportunistic and known to scavenge through human garbage. This bird is about 18–21 inches long. Pairs of ravens mate for life, and work together to construct an untidy bowl-shaped nest of sticks lined with grass and other soft materials. The raven is territorial, and when encountering intruders, will vocalize a loud warning or chase them away.

In some aboriginal traditions, the character Crow is a trickster figure, while the lore of the Noongar people says that these birds carry the spirits of the dead to the afterlife. Other Australians have nicknamed them "undertakers of the bush."

Many of the animals on O'Reilly covers are endangered; all of them are important to the world. To learn more about how you can help, go to *animals.oreilly.com*.

The cover image is from Wood's *Illustrated Natural History*. The cover fonts are URW Typewriter and Guardian Sans. The text font is Adobe Minion Pro; the heading font is Adobe Myriad Condensed; and the code font is Dalton Maag's Ubuntu Mono.

Learn from experts.
Find the answers you need.

Sign up for a **10-day free trial** to get **unlimited access** to all of the content on Safari,
including Learning Paths, interactive tutorials, and curated playlists that draw
from thousands of ebooks and training videos on a wide range of topics,
including data, design, DevOps, management, business—and much more.

Start your free trial at:

oreilly.com/safari

(No credit card required)

Milton Keynes UK
Ingram Content Group UK Ltd.
UKHW012036270824
447508UK00009B/185